# Chose Herself

shell.chelle

Chose Herself
shell.chelle

Book & Cover Design: Integrative Ink
www.integrativeink.com

shell.chelle.poetry@gmail.com

Poetry about a girl.
Just a girl,
Living her life.
Writing down her dreams.
Just a girl.
Imperfect and flawed.
Found her love,
Inside of herself.
Writing some words.
Words that became poetry.

These words became a story.
Her Story.
A story of a girl who:

*Lost Herself*

*Found Herself*

Then learned to...

*Love Herself*

In order to...

*Empower Herself*

And finally...

*Chose Herself*

This little side note:

This is her experience.
Her point of view.
Her feelings.
Her perspective.
Her story of letting go.
Her story of leaving,
A world of black and white.
Leaving the darkness,
And finding her light.
Her story of arriving,
To where the grey area resides.
This place of surrender.
This place of light.
A story of her memory.
A story of her truth.
A story from her eyes.
A story from her heart.
A story from her mind.
A story that she remembers,
As she listened to herself.
As she listened on her path.
Her path to self-love.
Her path to self-worth.
Her path to authenticity.
Her path to alignment.
Her path to her soul.
Her path.
Her love.
This is her story.

Also, this.
(In very fine print.)

These words.
These are just words.
Words of poetry.
Poetry to read.
These are just words.
Beautiful words.
Words of poetry.

# Chose Herself

## Make A New Choice

Make a new choice.
Choose again.
Making a new choice.
Choosing to get out of that loop.
That loop that you are in.
That loop,
Going around and around.
Making that same choice.
That same choice...
Over and over again.
Making a new choice,
Will feel uncomfortable.
Move into this discomfort.
Stay here.
Go into that unknown.
This new choice,
Will bring about change.
This new choice,
Will change who you are.
Little by little.
Each choice you make.
Choose again.
Choose different.
Choose different this time.
What will happen?
Happen with this choice.
Face that unknown.
This choice you will make.
Different this time.
Leave that loop.

That is the pattern,
Leave what you know.
That loop,
Is keeping you.
Keeping you from your pain.
You are disconnected.
Disconnected from your body.
Disconnected from your heart.
Get out of that loop.
Those limiting beliefs,
Over and over.
You hear them play.
Play in your head.
So engrained.
Make a new choice.
Create a new pathway.
Oh,
Wow this discomfort.
Let yourself feel it,
With each new choice...
It will bring that discomfort.
Get out of that pattern,
You went back to that loop...
Over and over...
Don't you want out?
Choose again.
Keep choosing different.
Until you feel your intuition.
Your intuition will guide you.
Once you get out of that loop.
That rumination.
Over and over...

Around in circles.
This loop took you over.
This loop takes you away.
Away from your light.
Away from your own voice.
Away from your calling.
Away from your intuition.
Get out of that loop.
Choose again...
This time,
Choose you.

## Out Of The Trenches

Out of the trenches.
Out she crawls.
Out of those trenches.
Those ditches.
She was laying in…
Covered in mud.
Covered in dirt.
Laying there,
In those trenches.
Trying to figure out…
Her way out.
How to get out?
Does she crawl?
Does she stand up?
Does she walk?
Does she run?
She didn't have the strength to stand up.
She couldn't stand…
Not yet.
She just needed rest.
She needed to just lay there.
Lay down…
Be here.
Be down there.
In these trenches.
She stayed down there.
Just rest.
Just stay.
Just cry.
Just be.

Just grieve.
Just don't give up.
Not giving up...
Just taking a break.
Making a new choice,
To stay.
Stop running.
Stop doing.
Stop going.
Always on the go.
Always deciding.
Always choosing.
Always moving.
Making a new choice.
Just stay.
Time to rest.
Time to recharge.
This rebirth.
This new choice.
Stay here in the trenches.
It's not pretty down here.
Covered in tears.
Covered up.
Feeling emotions.
Rest and sleep.
Healing and reflecting.
Soul searching.
Down here in these trenches.
This drain in her body.
She feels it leaving.
She feels it releasing.
Her body is reviving.

Ascension and rising.
Her new choices...
Brought her to herself.
Home to herself.
In these trenches.
She makes the choice...
She will crawl out.
She will crawl...
Slow and steady.
Peaceful and slow.
Regain her strength.
Her power will come when she stands up.
She stands up, holding her power.
She takes a step...
And walks forward.
These steps she takes,
As she walks away.
Confident and blissful.
Without a care in the world.
Shrugging off the chaos.
Shrugging off the dirt.
Shrugging off the mud.
Her steps she makes,
As she walks away.
Walks away towards a new choice.

## Not Where You Came From

I will choose differently.
Choose differently than how I was brought up.
I will choose discomfort,
Over feeling comfortable.
Where I feel comfortable,
Is not what is safe for me.
My comfort is not where I belong.
I need to create a new comfort zone.
What is in my blood...
What I was taught...
Question it all.
Question society.
Question beliefs.
Question your psyche.
Question why.
Why am I doing,
Exactly what I do?
Why am I constantly busy,
Or need all kinds of plans?
Why am I running around going...
Why am I the way I am?
Why don't I want to do that thing?
Why don't I want to do something different?
Why do I want to stay the same?
Why do I get the same kind of coffee?
Why do I keep going to the same exact place?
Why do I do the things I do?
Why am I around the people I choose?
Question it all...
No matter what.

Even if you love it,
Question it.
Ask Why.
Why a million times.
Why choose this?
Why choose that?
Why am I doing this?
Those questions will lead you.
Lead you to challenge yourself.
Challenge everything you know...
Challenge everything you don't.
Learn new ways.
Learn new things.
Learn something new,
Every day.
Talk to a stranger.
Be vulnerable and open.
Go to a new place.
Sit down a new way.
Get a new flavor of ice cream...
Just because.
Go buy some random flower seeds...
Just because you can.
Help the person next to you,
And cheer on that girl.
Cheer her on because she spoke up.
People watch and learn.
Learn from them.
Open your eyes.
Open your mind.
You can be anything...

Anything you want.
Anything you become...
You are not where you came from.

# Returned Back Home

She built her life,
Just the way she wants it.
She built her life,
By making new choices.
She built her life...
By becoming herself.
She became her true self,
When she found her love.
She believed in her worth.
She started using her voice.
She started seeing clearly,
Without those rose-colored glasses.
She walked towards peace.
She sat in the serenity.
She found her quiet place.
She returned back home.
Home to herself.
She cried the tears.
She fell to the ground.
She collected her tools.
She stopped sacrificing herself.
She started choosing.
Choosing herself.
Choosing what she wants.
Choosing what she doesn't...
Walking away from chaos.
Walking away from noise.
Walking away from ego.
Walking away from games.
She chose herself.

She chose her intuition.
She listened every time.
She had to take herself away.
She had to figure out her dreams.
She had to figure out her beliefs.
She had to put down dependency.
Dependency on others.
She had to go into her void.
She had to face her demons.
She had to peel back each layer.
Peel them away,
Until she became light.
So, light she could float.
Choosing for herself.
These new choices that she makes.

# The Truth Hurts

The truth hurts, right?
Hearing words you don't want to hear.
You hate the teller.
That truth teller.
Remember your haters,
Are really your lovers.
Envious and jealous.
Jealous of your truth.
Your authenticity.
Your aura.
Your love.
The truth comes out.
Those words you have been running from.
Those words.
That truth.
You really want to avoid.
Avoid what I am saying.
It is easier to deflect.
It is easier to move on.
Move forward.
Push it down.
"That truth you say...
No, I will just push it away.
Turn you into the bad one.
Turn you into the villain.
You spoke the truth.
Shame on you.
I am not the one with the problem.
I will always blame you.
Accountability is not in my psyche.

---

Self-reflection is impossible.
Impossible for me.
I wear rose-colored glasses,
And carry around a broom.
Sweeping everything away.
These words you say.
Just sweep.
Sweep.
Sweep.
Bury it away.
I will not admit.
Admit to what you say.
I will not learn from it.
I will just avoid these words.
These words you speak.
Turn it around on you,
Because it is never me.
Turn you into the villain,
Because you spoke the truth."

## This Gift Of Trust

She lost trust in herself.
She lost her trust.
She had to rebuild it.
Rebuild it piece by piece.
She played the victim for a little while.
Putting the blame on others...
Until she found herself again.
Built herself back up.
Built her trust back.
She gave herself this gift.
This gift of trust.
Choosing this for herself.
Inside of this choice.
This trust that she found.
She found her intuition.
She listened to it.
She became awakened,
And made a commitment.
This commitment to herself.
That she would never again...
Sacrifice herself.
She would honor herself,
With this gift.
This gift of trust.
Trust for herself.
Trusting and accepting.
Believing and hoping.
This gift came.
Came in the quiet,
As she left the noise.

Sitting in the solace,
Embracing her bliss.
Holding herself.
Holding her emotions.
Holding her heart.
Speaking her truth.
Making new choices.
Finding a new way.
Removing her walls,
As she learned to stay.

# Release Of My Grief

Shedding these tears.
These tears are for you.
These tears are my old life leaving.
Leaving me.
These tears,
They stream.
They are rolling down my face.
These tears are grief.
Grief for my old life.
These tears,
I shed.
I shed them as a release.
Releasing the old,
To embrace the new.
Releasing who I was,
To be who I am now.
Releasing these roles.
These roles I played.
These tears are for all of the times,
My love was shut down.
These tears are for every time,
I did not love myself.
These tears are for every time,
I did not choose myself.
These tears are for the memories I remember...
The good.
The bad.
Everything in between.
Let them pass.
Pass through me,

These tears are the release.
The release of my grief,
Of the love I once had.
These tears.
This wave.
This wave of grief.
It has arrived just for it to leave.

# The Villain To You

I will need to be the villain.
That villain to you.
It's easier for me to be.
To be that villain.
So, it doesn't have to be you.
It is easier to pin that blame.
Put it on me,
Because I took it.
I carried it for years,
And never shared my truth.
Walking around afraid.
Afraid of you.
In order for me to share,
And speak my truth.
I know that I will be the villain.
The villain to you.
It is your defense mechanism,
So you don't look at yourself.
It is your defense.
Your coping mechanism.
So, you stay on your pedestal,
And not shed a tear.
No tears will be shed for me.
Your villain.
The villain of your life.
No tears will be shed,
For how you treated me.
Just so you can stay.
Stay on that pedestal.

So, you won't have to change.
So, you won't have to feel,
Or have a conversation.
A deep conversation.
It would require you to leave the surface.
I am okay with being this villain.
This villain to you.
I am okay with it,
Because this is my new role I take on.
To leave all my other roles behind,
I am okay with becoming the villain now.
Everything comes with a cost.
Everything has a price.
A price to pay.
Having my voice,
Speaking my truth.
The price I will pay is to become the villain.
The villain to you.
You may still be running.
Running from yourself,
But I have stopped running.
I have learned to stay.
Stay,
And speak my truth.
Connected to my body.
Connected to my feelings.
Put my masks down.
I put them at your feet.
I set it all down,
Right at your feet.
I pick up my new role now...

As the villain.
I become this,
As I walk away.

# Why Did You Leave?!

Preparing for the worst.
Have a backup plan.
Something will happen.
Someone will turn on you.
Someone will stab you.
Stab you in the back.
Have a backup plan.
Because...
Hey,
You never know.
Walking on eggshells,
Every single day.
Don't disappoint them,
Okay?
They have high expectations.
Expectations of you.
They can throw their emotions at you,
Anytime they want.
They will turn the story around...
They turn it around on you.
You will be the bad one.
You will be blamed.
You better perform.
Give them their pretty words.
Keep yourself small,
And never speak up.
Be on,
Always on.
Be perfect.
Look your best.

Push your feelings down,
And put your best face on.
Don't change or become different...
Everything has a label.
Good or bad.
Black or white.
You are either difficult,
Or not enough.
You are overly sensitive,
Or way too much.
They won't tell you anything.
Because "You always have an emotion."
You are not allowed to have emotions...
Only they can.
You must be there for their emotions,
And fix every problem.
You are the fixer,
The problem solver.
The lifter.
The doer,
Get everything done.
All with a smile on your face,
Proving to them that you are the worthy one.
Doing for them,
So that they give you love.
God forbid,
If you stop and rest.
"Come on... get back up and do it all over again."
Repeat this daily,
This is your life.
You are on a leash.
This leash of control.

---

Cheer them back up,
Make everything better.
Sweep it under the rug.
Pretend nothing is wrong,
Even when you are dying inside.
Partake in the gossip with them,
Because the focus is never on them.
They avoid all of their problems,
And vulnerability.
Laugh it off and humor...
At inappropriate times.
Remember...
They like to put on the show.
Don't you love this black or white world...
Why did you leave?!

## Bury It Deep Down

Pushing it down.
Pushing it aside.
Push it over.
Bury it deep down.
Keep it covered up.
Keep it so far down.
So far down that you don't feel it.
Look at it...
See it.
Know it...
This grief will wait and wait,
Until you are ready to welcome it.
It will not go away.
It will just keep rising until you have the tools.
It is waiting for you.
This heaviness.
This confusion.
These heart wrenching cries.
This pain in your chest.
The sickness that comes,
Like you just want to throw up.
This exhaustion you feel.
It needs to be felt.
It needs to be seen.
Pushing it down,
Only prolongs it.
Pushing it away,
Only tucks it away...
Tucks it away for another day.
Another day that will come too soon.

You will have to commit to feel it.
This heaviness...
This is your grief,
It has arrived again.

# Emotional Intelligence

I am ultra-sensitive.
I can feel your unawareness.
I am sensitive to your emotions,
If you are unaware of them.
I am a sensitive soul,
Who knows what you are feeling.
I can feel what you feel,
Inside of my body.
So, if you are acting from unawareness,
I will know.
You must have emotional intelligence,
So that you can be aware.
Aware of this emotion.
This emotion in you.
It triggers me,
When you are unaware.
If you are walking around,
Throwing your emotions at everyone else.
Your emotional intelligence,
Will tell you the story.
The story of your emotions,
If you learn to listen.
Your emotional intelligence is your map.
It is your map to healing.
Healing yourself.
Your emotional intelligence will be your guide.
Your guide to your inner world.
Everything inside of your inner world,
It all will tell you.
Tell you a story.

Your emotions will guide you,
Just soften into them.
Let them rise,
Let them up.
Let them flow,
And then let them go.
Your body is your temple.
Your body holds this system.
Your system of emotions,
That flow throughout you.

## Broken By Them

At the end of the day,
When it is all said and done...
My parents broke my heart.
Both of them,
One by one.
My mom, at 14.
She tried to make it up.
Make it up when I was an adult...
But the damage was done.
She broke my heart.
I was 14.
She kicked me out,
And removed me.
Removed me from her life.
Removed me from my life.
Removed me,
Just like that.
Blamed it on me,
Because I was "bad."
She threw me away...
Tossed me out.
My first broken heart,
Shattered by my mom.
My dad broke my heart,
Every time he wouldn't listen to me.
He didn't hear me.
He didn't believe me,
When I tried to tell the truth.
He broke my heart a final time.
He turned on me,

Just like that.
He turned on me,
When he was all that I had.
He was the man.
The man in my life.
The man I looked up to.
The man I held up.
I held him up on a pedestal.
I relied on him.
I had trust in him.
He spoke some words,
To tear me down.
He spoke some words,
That broke my heart.
He made his choice,
To belittle me.
Both my parents left me...
Left me for their spouse.
Both of my parents...
Chose themselves.
They chose themselves,
Over me.
They made their choice,
I see it now.
I understand now,
That they only did what they knew.
But it doesn't change,
This sadness I feel.
I understand now.
I see it clear.
My first broken heart came from my mom.
My dad was the final break.

A parent's job is to love.
It is not to tear their child down.
Let's stop pretending...
That it never happened.
Let's stop seeing it,
From just their perspective.
I have a perspective too...
But they did not care about that.
My perspective did not matter...
Because it was all about them.
Shoved to the side,
As I care for them.
Prove who I am,
To receive love from them.
A parent's job is to care.
It is not to cause pain or a tear.
A tear in my heart.
One,
That I have been trying to mend.
My heart was broken.
Broken by them.

## Her Beauty Was Back

This beautiful wildflower.
She sits in this peace.
This peaceful place.
This peaceful field.
This field of green.
Weeds and grass.
Growing strong,
After the storms.
These storms rolled in,
And blew her down.
Wilted for a while.
Her strength was gone.
Her beauty was taken,
Or so she thought.
This false story,
She told herself.
This story was not true.
This storm brought these stories.
These stories she believed.
These stories to undo.
This unraveling.
This erasing.
This complete revision.
Everything inside of her,
Will be renewed.
This death in these storms,
While she was wilting.
Wilting without her strength.
Wilting without her replenishment.
Wilting in this environment.

This environment she knew.
This rebirth.
This recharge.
This revision.
This clarity.
This revival.
This beauty.
She came alive,
After the storm.
This storm that came.
These repeated storms,
That came to blow her away.
Her roots were strong.
She stayed grounded.
Grounded in herself,
As she remembered.
Remembered who she was,
And to never give up.
She allowed herself to wilt.
She allowed herself to rest.
She surrendered to the storm,
And allowed herself to fall.
It's okay to go down.
It's okay to not stand tall.
It's okay to wilt,
While you fall.
Her stem was shaken.
She shed her skin.
Her leaves were gone.
So was her bloom.
Her beautiful colors blew right off her stem.
Her flower.

---

Her bloom,
Blew away.
She knew she would never be the same.
She knew it would take time,
To grow these back.
Grow new leaves.
Her skin would be renewed.
She knew she would bloom.
Bloom again.
She knew it would take time.
Time to renew.
Time to bloom.
Time to be whole again.
Her whole flower.
Her whole stem.
Her beautiful bloom.
Her beauty in this field,
Would show again.
She just needed time,
After these storms.
Little by little,
Her new skin.
Her new leaves.
Shades of green.
Her stem thickened.
Her roots expanded,
As her insides changed.
Her insides changed so she could stand tall.
New growth.
Her colors.
These vibrant colors.
Her bloom.

Her flower,
Back again.
More beautiful than ever,
Her beauty was back.

# Mend

My heart hurt so much,
That I shut it off.
I shut it down.
My heart,
This crack.
It tore me up,
To watch you the way you were.
I put up a façade,
Because I needed to survive.
I needed to breathe.
I needed to live.
I did it for me,
But also for you.
I couldn't enable you...
I needed to stop.
The only way I knew how,
Was to shut down my heart.
Block it all out,
I won't cry at all.
I won't shed a tear,
I will become cold.
Cold and heartless,
Is what I became.
That was my façade...
It was what I had to do.
It was what I had to do,
To not feel the hurt.
That throbbing hurt,
My heart aching and burning.
Breaking.

It was broken.
It was shattered into pieces.
I would just pick myself back up,
I needed to build up my strength.
Before I could begin to feel.
Feel this hurt I had for you.
Feel this pain.
So painful it was for me to let you go.
Shut that door...
That door on you.
Your beautiful soul wasn't there anymore.
Your beautiful soul was covered.
Covered by pain.
Pain that was being projected.
Projected out onto me.
I couldn't make you see.
I just knew I had to leave.
Leave you to mend your wounds.
Leave you so that I could mend mine.

# I Did It For Us

I put up that façade,
Because it hurt me too much.
It hurt me too much,
To cry these tears.
These tears of love.
This love I had for you.
I had this love for the life that I had built.
I built it with you.
I put up that façade,
Because I just wanted to hold you.
I wanted to love you.
I wanted to but couldn't.
I had to go.
I had to leave you,
So that you could take care of yourself.
I had to leave you,
So that you could love yourself.
I had to leave,
For me.
For myself.
I had to leave,
To take care of myself.
I needed to leave…
I did it for us.

# Running Into The Arms Of Other Men

I was running into the arms of other men...
Hoping they would be you.
Each time,
They would be you.
Comparing and comparing to what we had.
The good times we had.
The love we shared...
I was holding onto that,
So that I couldn't move on.
Just keep holding on...
Holding onto you.
Running into the arms of other men...
Hoping and hoping,
I could just move on...
Without feeling this pain.
This pain inside.
I wasn't able to move on,
Because I hadn't let you go.
I was still holding on.
Holding onto you.
Running into the arms of other men...
Hoping to feel safe,
Like I once did.
Like I once did with you...
I once felt safe.
I felt safe in your embrace.
In your arms.
Running for safety,
Into the arms of other men.
All because I didn't want to feel,

This pain inside.
I once felt safe.
Safe in your arms.
What I would give,
To feel this again.
I needed to grieve.
Grieve my safety.
My safety I would feel,
In your arms.

## I Give Up All Of This

I give up all of this.
I surrender it all.
I give it all up,
So that I can fall.
So that I can fly.
Soar with the wind.
Fly with my wings.
This freedom came.
Came at a cost.
It cost me my all,
Cost me my tears,
So much sadness.
Let go of it all,
As I let it all go.
Let it all fall.
Fall off of me,
Spreading my love.
I spread it through the air,
As I fly free.
I let it all go,
As tears stream down my face.
Tears fill my eyes,
As I look behind.
I look back and see…
I understand it all.
It makes sense to me now.
This clarity came…
And cost me my all.
Everything I built.
Everything I loved.

I give it all up,
So that I can fly free.
I leave it all behind,
As I fly with the wind.
This wind lifts me up.
Lifts me above,
All that I was.
Lifts me above,
Everything I built.
I soar above it all,
As I leave it all behind.
This wind lifts me up,
As I spread my wings.
I look down below me,
Flying through the sky.
I look down below me,
At everything I built.
Everything I built,
It is gone now.
I set it all free,
I let it all go.
I soar above it all,
I am free.

# I Wanted To Go To You

So many times,
I wanted to go to you.
Have you comfort me.
Have you hold me.
So many times,
I wanted to go to you.
See you.
Look at you,
In your eyes.
But the person I wanted.
He was gone.
He couldn't hold me.
He couldn't protect me.
That guy was gone.
The eyes I wanted.
Those eyes weren't yours.
Those eyes were glazed over.
Those eyes weren't comfort.
Comfort to me…
Not anymore.
Those arms that I wanted.
Wanted to hold me,
Those arms weren't able to…
Hold me anymore.
That guy,
I loved.
He needed himself.
He needed his love.
He needed him.

He couldn't give it to me.
I gave myself away...
I drained myself,
Just to save him.
Trying to run.
Run after him.
Run after him,
As he neglected himself.
Abandoning himself.
Running away,
As I was running after him.
Trying so hard.
Too hard that I left...
I left myself.
I left her with nothing.
I left her alone,
Without my love.
Because I was running after him,
To give it to him.
So many times,
After you left...
I wanted to go to you,
Just to hold you.
Hold you and love you and comfort you,
Be with you.
But I had to shut my heart down.
I shut it all down,
Because I didn't know how to stop enabling you.
I couldn't hold you.
I couldn't love you.
I couldn't comfort you,

Or be with you.
Because I needed to do this all...
For myself.

## Your Insecurity Is Showing.

I See your insecurity,
I feel it coming out.
It is here.
It is blatantly showing.
Showing itself.
You really can't hide it.
It is showing it's face.
You are not owning it.
You are not acknowledging it.
You are not looking at it.
You are not feeling it.
You are shoving it away...
So, it is projecting out.
Out,
My way.
It is showing.
It is showing.
I see it so clear.
I don't take it personal,
Because I know it is not me.
Jealousy.
Envy.
Whatever it is...
Your insecurity is showing.
It is glowing.
It is here.

# Her Paper Of Healing

She put her heart down on paper,
To get this pain out of her.
To help make her heart whole again.
She shares her tears...
They are all out.
Out on these pages.
She writes about her grief.
These words of grief on this paper.
She explains it all.
She shares it all.
She describes her sadness.
She describes her fall.
Her fall into the darkness,
Into the depths.
She shares the absolute ugliness...
How she turns it into beauty.
She shares her alchemy,
Her transformation.
She shares how she finds her clarity,
Deep in the confusion.
She shares her heartbreak.
Her walls coming down.
She shares her inner world.
She shares her sorrow.
She shares her shadow.
She shares it all on paper.
This paper became a map.
Her bible.
Her temple.
Her love.

Her map.
Because she found her love,
Inside of her healing.
She followed her map.
Her internal map.
Her internal compass,
Which led the way.
She wrote these words.
She wrote them down.
Down on paper,
Covered in tears.
She wrote them in the darkness,
With glimpses of light.
This paper of words.
Her words.
This paper became,
Her paper of healing.

## Subservient

You want subservient.
Subservient out of me.
You want me to obey.
Obey your rules.
You want me to listen.
Listen to you.
You want to control me.
Yeah,
No thanks.
You want subservient.
You want small.
You want me to fall.
Fall at your commands.
You want me at your beckon call.
You want what you want.
But no,
That's not me.
You want me to cower.
Cower down.
You want me to be submissive.
Submissive to your control.
You want me to bow down.
Bow down to your ego.
You want power over me.
You want to quiet my voice.
You want me to sit there and look pretty,
While I allow you to walk on me.
You want me to respect you,
While you disrespect me.
You want me to shut down,

And not allow me to speak.
You want this subservient behavior.
You want this from me,
But you will not be getting any of that.
Not out of me.
You want to throw those knives,
While I play your game.
You want me to keep coming back,
As I shove myself aside.
You want this subservient girl,
Who gives up her power.
You won't be challenged.
You refuse to be wrong.
You want to push my buttons,
And bother me.
Get that reaction...
Reaction out of me.
I am done reacting.
I accept you for you,
As I leave you over there.

## Let It Play Out

Let it play out.
Play out like it will.
Let it play out.
Play out the way it should.
It will play out,
Just the way it is supposed to.
Let it play out.
Just let it all be.
Let everything go.
Let yourself lead.
Lead the way.
Follow your heart,
By choosing yourself.
Choose you,
No matter what.
You are important.
You are it.
You are beautiful.
You are you.
You are incredible.
You are light.
You are peaceful.
Sitting there.
Nothing to do.
Just be.
Nothing to prove.
Just see.
See yourself,
Just as you are.
Rest.

Just rest.
That is all.
Surrender yourself.
Trust and have faith.
It will all play out,
Just as it will.

## This Chosen Spot

This undoing.
This unravel.
This,
Leaving what you know.
This new chapter.
This start again.
This forgetting what you know.
This reprogramming.
This recharge.
This walking away.
This clearing.
This cleansing.
This shedding everything.
This leaving behind,
What isn't yours.
This listening to your inner voice.
This doing what you want.
This going wherever you go.
This listening to your needs.
This going to where you belong.
This leaving where you no longer fit.
This growing into a wildflower.
This wildflower,
On your own.
This spiritual awakening.
This consciousness.
This path.
This journey.
This opening your heart.
This finding your light.

---

This empowerment.
This introduction to your soul.
This authenticity.
This chosen spot.
The chosen spot,
Is you.

## Triggered.

This anger.
These voices.
This sadness.
This reaction.
These tears.
This tantrum.
This inappropriate reaction.
These flashbacks.
I am triggered,
By the past.
My past is here.
It is not you.
This trigger is my teacher.
This trigger is my wound.
This is me having a moment.
This moment of my past.
I am triggered.
Give me a minute.
Give me a second.
Let me think.
Let me be in this.
Let me sit in this.
I know this is me.
I am triggered.
I am affected.
This moment...
Oh wow.
This trigger brought me back.
Back to that old world.
Oh wow...

Like I am re-living it again.
I know just what this is.
This trigger…
I am triggered.
Give me a minute.
Let me calm myself down,
This is intense.
I need to regulate myself.
Breathe in.
Breathe out.
Deep breaths will relax me.
Pass through this moment.
This moment I am living.
I am calm now.
This trigger has passed.
It doesn't last.
Just let it come,
And just let it go.
It is gone now.
I am fine now.

## This Disrespect

This disrespect.
Blatant disrespect.
Here it is,
And you don't see...
You blame it on me.
How can you not see?
This blatant disrespect,
That you are throwing right at me.
You say you would never...
Disrespect me.
But you did.
Continuously.
You say you care...
And your way of showing this...
Is blatant disrespect.
So, you can be in control.
You call the shots.
You don't like it?
That I am standing up for myself...
Oh,
You don't like it now?
That I see you.
I see exactly what is happening...
And I call it out.
Because I am putting an end to this.
This blatant disrespect.
This belittlement.
Would you act this way towards another man?
If a man was standing in front of you...
Or is it because I am a female?

*& I am beneath you...*
This easy target...
Just put her down.
"Please sit down.
I'm too busy right now.
Too busy for you.
When I get time...
I will do it on my terms,
Because I am in control."
This belittlement.
This blatant disrespect.
I am done with it.

# These Dreams

Oh,
These dreams.
These dreams I have.
I pray every day.
I pray for these dreams.
Oh,
These dreams.
These dreams I have.
I imagine this day,
That my dreams come true.
Little by little...
Patience and surrender.
It will all happen,
Just the way it's supposed to.
These dreams,
I can feel.
These dreams,
In me.
These dreams are mine.
They will come true.
I feel this in my bones.
I feel this in my soul.
I feel this in my heart.
As I imagine this dream.
This dream,
Coming true.
I hold onto hope.
I hold onto faith.
I will live my life,
In this space.

---

This space of waiting.
This space of peace.
So calm.
So quiet.
Nothing to do.
Boredom.
Relaxing.
A lot of rest.
Grieving my identity.
All of who I was.
Grieving myself.
I am not her anymore.
Just a girl...
Having these dreams.
These dreams are who I am now.
I let everything else go.
I hold onto nothing...
As I see my dreams.

## Imperfect

Embrace that imperfection.
Embrace those flaws.
Embrace that uncertainty.
Embrace what could go wrong.
Leave it as it is,
There is beauty in that flaw.
Leave it just as it is,
Own it as it is.
Own that it's not perfect.
Own that it's not correct.
Own that the mistake was made,
And move on to what is next.
Perfection doesn't exist.
Leave it as it is.
Accept that imperfection.
Accept those minor scrapes.
Accept those scars on you.
Accept that everything is,
Just as it's supposed to be.
Leave it all behind...
As you move forward.
Bring your flaws with you,
Along with your weaknesses.
You have learned to love them,
Through all the storms.
Those flaws are not who you are...
Just a minor part.
Those mistakes are forgotten about,
As you take steps forward.
Those mistakes don't matter.

What matters is you.
You matter.
Your heart.
Your love.
Your worth.
Your voice.
Your choice.
Your choice is you.
You matter,
No matter what.

# These Glimpses Of Love

These tears of joy.
Tears of gratitude.
Tears of safety.
Tears of feeling.
These tears for myself.
Look how far...
How far you have come.
Giving yourself love,
No matter what.
Loving yourself unconditionally.
Through the fog.
Through the hardships.
Through the fire.
Through the storms.
Being there.
Attending to,
Every single one of your needs.
Surrender and let go.
Be in this moment,
Even when it is hard.
Let the light in.
Even in the darkness.
Glimpses of light,
In the dark.
These glimpses,
Bring these tears.
These tears of joy.
These tears of gratitude.
How far you have come...
You have opened your heart.

Through the darkness.
Let this light in.
Let it in fully.
Do you see this beauty?
This beauty in this moment.
This beautiful moment.
This sound of silence.
Beauty surrounds you.
Do you see it?
Can you feel it?
These glimpses of beauty.
These glimpses of love.
Do you feel this love?

## She Just Is

This calm.
The water is calm.
There is no wind.
There is nothing to hear.
The sky.
The sky up above her.
These clouds up above.
These clouds are just there.
The sky is blue.
This baby, soft blue.
This silence.
This silence in the air.
The wildflowers are in full bloom.
Everywhere she looks...
The wildflowers are there.
The beautiful colors.
The colors of the blooms.
These wildflowers are her inspiration.
A seed planted.
A seed that blows.
A new growth here.
A new growth there.
Wherever they grow,
They grow.
The weather that comes.
The storms that arrive.
The winds that blow through.
The temperatures.
The darkness.
The light.

These wildflowers just are.
Just like her.
She just is.
Anywhere and everywhere.
She just is.

## Your Light Is On

Break that dynamic.
Break it now.
Break that codependency.
Break that attachment.
Break that disfunction.
Break that pattern.
Break those habits.
Break that cycle.
Break it all.
Be the cycle breaker.
Become the hated one.
Become the one they're jealous of.
Become the villain.
Become the authentic one.
Become the one who sets boundaries.
Become the one who does their own thing.
Become the one who rocks the boat.
Become your own energy.
Become exactly what you want to be.
Become the one who is no longer walked on.
Become the one who uses their voice.
Become the one who speaks their truth.
Become your own vibe.
Become whoever you are.
Whoever you are inside.
Your soul.
Become your soul.
Pure and clear.
Bright and light.

You are glowing.
Your light is on.

## This Direction

She knew what she wanted.
She knew where she was going.
She had no idea,
But she trusted in herself.
Trusted in her path.
Her intuition would tell her.
She trusted in her faith.
The faith in her.
She was connected.
Connected to her soul.
She knew right where she needed to go.
She had no idea where that even was.
But it was a feeling.
A feeling she knew.
A feeling she trusted.
She knew.
She finally knew.
She was lost for a while.
Lost and wandering...
She feared the unknown.
She finally trusted.
Trusted her fear.
Her fear would lead her.
Guide her,
And push her.
Push her in the direction.
This direction for her.
Her fear was her inspiration.
This inspiration in her.

# Holding This Moment

She is holding this moment.
This moment right now.
This joy.
This bliss.
This moment is hers.
She is holding this.
Nothing else,
But this.
This,
In her hands.
This,
In her heart.
This,
In her aura.
She is holding this.
Pure bliss.
She holds onto it.
Holding it lightly...
Not too tight.
Her grip is free.
This moment is fleeting.
This moment won't come again.
She is soaking in it.
This moment,
Is hers.
This moment,
She holds.

# Retreat

Retreat into your space...
Into your bubble.
Into your world,
Into yourself.
Retreat into quiet.
Into solitude and peace.
Retreat and leave.
Leave the chaos.
Leave the noise.
Leave the energy.
The energy that is not yours.
The energy that is taking from you.
Retreat into yourself.
Retreat into your body.
Retreat into your mind.
Meet that mind/body connection.
You cannot find it anywhere outside.
Outside of you.
Nothing to find on the outside world.
It is all inside.
Once you create your inner world.
Just the way you want it...
You become a magnet.
You will attract what you are.
Nothing to do.
Nowhere to go.
Retreat into yourself.
Retreat into peace.
Retreat into light.
Retreat into love.

---

Retreat into vibrance.
Retreat into your soul.
Retreat into you...
Into who you really are.

# Hold Yourself Up

Follow that drive.
That drive in you.
Follow that deep inner knowing.
That inner knowing that you know.
Follow that feeling.
That feeling in your gut.
Follow your heart.
That pounding in your heart.
Follow your vision.
That vision in your mind.
Follow the sensations.
The sensations in your body.
Follow your breath.
Your breath knows what is next.
Stay in this moment.
This moment right now.
The moment will come.
You will know when you know.
Your strength will come,
After you rest.
Your healing will arrive,
When you sit in the feelings.
Your light will take over,
After the darkness.
Your faith will carry you,
When you have nothing left.
Your love will arrive,
When you test your worth.
You will become who you are,
After you grieve who you were.

Your future will arrive,
When you let everything else go.
Your purpose is in you.
You just have to listen.
Your beauty is there,
Because of the ugliness.
Your trust will come,
After you fall.
Your vibrance will come over you,
After you shed your skin.
Your new skin is powerful,
You have earned it.
Peel back the layers,
Your soul is underneath.
Learn to love solitude.
Your intuition will speak.
It is in stillness,
That you find your wholeness.
Let it be quiet.
Let everything just be.
Walk away from the noise,
Those answers will come.
Have patience and just be.
Let everything just be.
Breathe in.
Breathe out.
Here you are.
Don't ever give up,
Even when hope is gone.
Let go of that hope,
New hope will come.
Loosen your grip,

Everything is not meant to stay.
Learn to let go,
And say goodbye.
Learn to accept,
And then to forgive.
There is always a way,
You just have to believe.
Keep your faith,
Hold yourself up.

## Just As It Should

When you have outgrown...
Outgrown where you are.
You will feel it.
This feeling takes you over.
Every single day.
When you have outgrown...
Outgrown your life.
You will feel it.
You can't control it.
This feeling will push you.
Push you out.
Out of this life.
This life that you are in.
Out of the way.
Out of your own way.
This feeling will guide you.
Guide you to what is right.
What is right for you?
You don't even know this yet...
You have no idea where you are going.
You have no idea where you will end up.
All you know is that you have outgrown where you are...
And it is getting really hard.
It is hard to be there every single day.
It is hard to wake up every single day.
It is hard to tolerate people every single day.
Because all you can feel...
Is this feeling inside.
It is taking you over.
It is becoming heavy.

It is becoming louder.
Louder each day.
Where to go now?
When do you go?
What is the next stop?
Who even knows...
Listen to your body.
Your body will tell you.
Trust in your intuition.
Let your intuition speak.
Let it lead the way.
Your intuition is in control.
For now,
Just be.
Just trust and be.
Waiting for something...
Waiting for a sign.
Waiting for what's next.
What's next for you?
Just trust and surrender,
And relax into this moment.
This moment is hard...
You are over it.
Just be here.
Be here now.
Everything will end up,
Just as it should.

## My Teacher

This is my teacher.
This is my lesson.
I am learning.
I am seeing.
I am hearing.
Seeing it all.
Hearing it all.
I understand.
This is my lesson.
Thank you,
My teacher.
This is goodbye.
This is detachment.
This is the let go.
Letting it all go.
Losing it all.
This is what it feels like.
This is my teacher.
This is showing...
Showing me my lessons.
My eyes are open.
Parting ways.
This no longer serves me.
I am not in alignment.
I am not where I belong.
This is not me...
Not anymore.
Grieving all that was...
And what used to be.
This is no longer...

No longer me.
This no longer fits.
Fits into my heart.
I have outgrown this.
I have detached.
Detached from this life.
Detached from this part.
This is no longer mine.
I need to say goodbye.
It is time.
Time to part ways.
This no longer aligns.
Aligns with my soul.

# Fall Off Of You

Letting go.
It sets you free.
Sets you apart.
Apart from what's not meant to be.
Letting go brings peace.
Peace to your heart.
Letting go brings you,
Straight to your dreams.
Let it all go.
Let it all fall.
Let it all just fall away.
It will all fall into place.
Right where you need it.
Where you need to go.
Right where you belong.
Right where you will grow.
But first...
Let it all go.
Let it all fall.
Fall right off you.
This is not yours.
Neither is this.
Get this away.
Walk away from this.
Put your foot down.
This is not right for you.
Move along.
Keep moving.
Keep going.
You are on your own now.

Just keep thriving.
Don't stop hoping.
Keep your faith.
Keep your heart open.
But let it all go...
It might not make sense,
But someday it will.
These tears will make sense...
So will this grief.
You have to grieve,
What will never be.
Just keep grieving,
And just let it all go.
Let it all fall.
Fall off of you.

## Crumbling Down

Crumbling down.
Crashing down.
Let your world just crash right down.
Let it all fall.
Fall away.
Let it all come crashing down.
Let it all fall.
Fall away.
This world is not yours.
Not anymore.
You are no longer connected.
Connected to it.
Detach.
Just you.
Watching your world,
Come crashing down.
You are not being seen.
Seen for who you are.
You are not being understood.
Understood for who you have become.
You are someone different.
You have shed it all.
Shed it away.
You are not her anymore.
This world crumbles,
At your feet.
Nothing left.
Take a seat.
Sit down and watch.

Watch it all...
Come crumbling down.

# Trust

Follow your heart.
Just trust it completely.
Wholeheartedly,
You are trusting.
Just trust in yourself.
Trust in your voice.
That inner voice.
The noise of the world,
No longer affects you.
Trust in your guidance.
Your intuition.
Trust in that feeling.
That feeling will lead you.
The noise and that chaos.
Everything is quiet.
Nothing to hear.
Nothing can affect you.
Follow and trust.
Surrender to this.
This feeling will lead you,
Into your world.
Your new world,
Where you belong.
That world is not here.
That world is not yours.
You sit there confused,
Disconnected and bored.
You are not connecting,
To your outside world.
You have found detachment.

You have found your love.
Your love in yourself.
Your love for your soul.

## The Last Straw

Falling down.
Falling off.
Crashing down.
Giving everything up.
One last straw.
That is it.
That's all it took.
That one last straw.
That is all I need.
This leap of faith.
That's all I see.
That one last straw.
That decision is made.
This all just pushed me.
Pushed me here.
Pushed me off.
Off of this cliff.
Pushed me,
To this decision.
This decision,
Is what is next.
One last straw.
That's all it took.
I am standing here,
Looking back.
I stop myself.
No more looking back.
Just stay right here.
Right here,
In this moment.

This moment,
Right now.
That is all I see.
That is all I need.
This moment I am in,
With this one last straw.

# Seen

She didn't feel seen.
Seen in her world.
She didn't feel seen,
By her own self.
She needed to see herself fully.
She needed to sit and love herself.
She needed to see.
See her wounds.
She needed to see.
See her life.
She needed to put effort in,
To see this big picture.
This big picture of her.
Ask herself questions...
"Why do you do this?
How?
What?
Where?
...and when?
When did this start?"
She will see it all.
She will understand.
She will change it all.
She will choose herself.
She is done putting herself last.
She is done,
Being walked on.
She realized she allowed this...
For way too long.
This was her way...

That people took advantage of.
They took advantage of her kindness.
They took advantage of her love.
She allowed this,
As they gave her their breadcrumbs.
She gave and gave...
Validation and support.
They gave her back breadcrumbs,
And ran away with her love.
This felt normal.
This was her normal.
Her familiar.
Her comfort.
She will let them show her.
Show her who they are.
She will let them show her,
Their true colors will come out.
But not anymore,
Will she allow this.
Being walked on.
Being talked down to.
Being stomped on and used.
Being taken advantage of.
Surrounding herself with takers...
She is done with the breadcrumbs.

# Get Real

Once you get real with yourself,
See yourself in all angles.
Once you shed so many layers.
Layers of skin of who you once were.
Once you give everything up.
Everything you knew.
Everything you loved.
Once you know grief,
Like you never knew it before.
Once you open the door,
To your inner world.
Once you put a foot in.
Take some steps forward.
Breathe in.
Breathe out.
A walk through the dark.
You see it all.
You have moved below the surface.
So much darkness.
Once you sort through it,
Pick up each piece.
Drop your illusion.
This illusion you see.
This illusion you saw through.
This lens.
This fog.
Once you shed your darkness,
Is when you find your light.
Once you walk away from all that you knew.
Once you see it for what it really is.

Once you have the guts,
To stand up for yourself.
Once you put yourself first.
Stop living for the world.
These expectations.
These societal beliefs.
Once you find your authenticity.
Once you do all of this.
You become so completely unstoppable.
You become so enriched.
So enhanced.
You become so confident in yourself.
So secure.
Secure with who you are.
Once you get real...
Get real with yourself.
Accept yourself,
Just as you are.
No more worries.
You don't care.
Live your life authentically.
You are free.

## Sometimes It's Time.

Sometimes it's time...
It's time to recharge.
It's time to drift apart.
Drifting close,
Then drifting away.
Everything changes.
Our lives,
They change.
Our needs,
They change.
Sometimes it's time...
Time to leave.
Time to drift.
Time to part ways.
Sometimes it's time...
Time to let go.
Let go of the grip.
Look away.
Find something new.
Something that lifts.
Something that lights you up.
Sometimes it's time...
Time for you.
Time for you to go be someone else.
Time for you to go someplace else.
Time for you to feed your soul.
Time for you to figure out what is next.
Sometimes it's time...
Time to drift.
Drifting apart.

Drifting away.
Drifting and drifting...
Sometimes it's time.

## Leave You Behind

You see that old version.
That old version of me.
You are seeing this old version...
Why can't you see?
Why can't you see this me that I am?
Why can't you see this me that I made?
Why can't you see this new version of me?
You keep searching to find that old me.
That old version of me,
You no longer can find.
That old version of me,
Is no longer there.
Keep searching.
Keep growing,
Until I am out of reach.
You are a new version of you...
I see you.
Why can't you see me?
I see you.
I see that new you.
Why can't you put the time in for me?
Why can't you see me?
I just don't understand.
It just wasn't meant to be...
For you to see me.
You were brought to me,
As a person on my path.
It is time for us to part ways now,
Because I need to be seen.
I need to be seen,

For this me that I am.
I can't pull myself back,
To that me that I was.
This me,
That was your friend.
This me,
That you see.
I just cannot go that way,
I must keep moving.
I see us,
Going in different directions.
Different ways.
Different paths.
I see you going over there.
I am over here,
Going down my own path.
I am bored with our conversations...
I am not lit up...
I am completely bored...
I have gone inside,
Deeper into myself.
You are living on the surface,
Doing different things.
Doing.
Doing.
Doing.
While I am,
Staying.
Staying.
Staying.
Finding my feelings,
While you suppress yours.

Living on the surface.
The conversations are fading.
You are lost in the noise.
You are lost in the doing.
Lost in the chaos...
While I am sitting.
Staying in the quiet.
Staying in the stillness.
Listening to the quiet.
These emotions I am feeling.
They are fleeting.
Finding clarity.
Clarity for my soul.
Manifesting connection.
Opening my heart.
Clearing and releasing,
As I find freedom.
I see myself drifting...
Drifting from you.
Drifting from a path,
We once walked together.
No longer feeling supported.
Supported by you.
No longer feeling lifted.
Lifted by you.
I no longer feel seen.
I no longer feel heard.
I no longer feel understood.
Understood by you.
Different worlds.
Different paths.
I feel myself giving.

Giving too much.
Giving and giving.
I am the giver.
I feel weighed down.
Weighed down by you.
I am making myself smaller.
Smaller for you.
Smaller to have you feel comfortable,
As I lift you higher.
I need to stop.
Stop making myself small.
It is time to lift myself up.
Lift myself higher...
And leave you behind.

## Too Well

She opened her heart.
She trusted and loved.
She relied on them.
They were her life.
She opened her soul.
She gave them her heart.
She gave and gave and gave...
And gave some more.
Until the day,
She opened her eyes.
She saw the mistreatment.
She saw the betrayal.
She saw the pile.
The pile they swept away,
Like it never happened.
Like it didn't even happen.
She saw the dismissal.
She saw how it was.
She thought this was normal,
Until she saw.
She saw the reality,
Without the illusion.
She realized her worth,
When the illusion fell off.
She realized the love that she knew...
Was never really love at all.
She had opened her heart,
To hurt and pain.
She opened herself up,
To people she loved.

People she knew well.
People who took off.
They took off and left...
And stole her heart.
She gave them her heart,
Without wanting anything in return...
Unconditional love is what she gave.
All of her love,
She gave away.
Until the day...
The day she changed.
The day she realized,
She needed this love.
This love was for herself,
And she was giving it all away.
This day,
Was her commitment.
Her commitment to herself.
This day,
Was the day she would choose herself.
She opened herself up,
And thought she was safe.
What she knew was safety,
Was really a cage.
This cage that kept her,
As a possession.
A possession to them,
That they could stomp on and use.
A possession to them,
That they could hurt and betray.
A possession to them...
A place to dump on.

---

Dump all of their own hurt and pain.
It was all of their pain that she took on.
She carried it for them,
Because she thought this was her job.
She thought this was her purpose.
She did this for them,
Because she had love for them.
She was this possession to them.
This possession,
That they never truly saw.
They never saw her,
For who she really was.
Because all they saw her as,
Is what she could do for them.
If she couldn't be used...
Used for their needs.
If she couldn't be of value...
Value to them...
She would be scolded,
Or she would be left.
Punished and abandoned.
These words she knew well.
These words brought her to find forgiveness.
She must find forgiveness in order to accept.
Accept this is the way...
The only way she knew.
She knew this way...
This way too well.
She promised herself,
She would find a new way.
She did for them....
Until the day she stopped.

She carried their burdens,
Until she put them all down.
She finally found her way...
This was the day,
She finally found *her* crown.

# Open

This is not what I want.
This is not normal.
This is not how I like to feel.
This is not me.
Open your mind.
Open your heart.
Open the world.
So many options.
So many choices.
Make the changes.
Close the business.
Write the book.
Travel east.
Travel south.
Travel anywhere.
That new song.
This new place.
These new people.
Lose the fear,
And keep your faith.
Learn to let go.
Let go of it all.
New.
New.
New.
Everything is new.
Be brave.
Take a breath.
Breathe in.
Breathe out.

Surrender and trust.
Learn to be an outcast.
You are not here to fit in.
Learn to be different.
You don't need to be liked.
You will piss people off,
When you become who you are.
You are not what society says.
You are not what anyone says.
You are who you say,
And that's just how it is.
Your authenticity will shine.
Shine so bright.
It will blind who is not coming.
Coming with you on your path.
Your light will lead you,
To where you have to go.
Walking away from what dims you.
Figuring it out,
On your own.
Leaving the noise.
Getting quiet.
Quiet with yourself.
Quiet with your heart.
Finding your way.
Finding your path.
Listening to your intuition,
As you hear the signs.

# They Don't See You

When people don't see you.
They really don't see you.
They are so wrapped up.
Wrapped up in their own life.
They see you...
Just a glimpse.
Just a glimpse of you.
But they don't really want to know you.
The depths of you.
They really can't see you.
See the real you.
The whole you.
All parts of you.
They really don't know.
They don't know you.
They don't understand,
They are just so wrapped up.
Wrapped up in a world.
A world full of noise.
Wrapped up in a world.
A world of illusions.
Happiness and smiles.
Validation and goodness.
They don't take the time.
The time to really see you.
They can't see you,
Like you see them.
You see them deeply,
On a deeper level.
You see through the barriers.

You see through the walls.
You see past the surface,
Because that is who YOU are.
They cannot see.
Past their walls.
They cannot see,
Past their illusion.
They cannot see,
Past the surface.
Because you can only meet them,
Where they are at.
How deeply they have gone into themselves.
That is where you meet them.
That is where you will stay.
You meet them there.
You see them there.
They can't see you,
Because they are staying back there.
Back there as you go deeper.
Deeper into the layers.
Peeling back each layer.
Each layer that is there.
They can't see you,
Because they have stopped peeling the layers.
This is their comfort.
Their comfort is there.
They can't see you,
Because of how deeply you have gone.
They just can't see you.
This is something you must accept.
You have to accept this as you move deeper.
You have to accept this as you move forward.

You see yourself.
You choose yourself.
You understand these layers.
You understand this depth.
Deeper and deeper.
Further you go,
Peeling back those layers...
Until you become whole.
Your ego is gone.
And it is just your heart.
Your heart is beating.
Those layers are gone.
They can't see you,
Because they are covered in walls.
They just can't see you.
They don't know you anymore...

## ...How Could You?

They didn't see her.
They didn't see her emotions.
They didn't see how they affected her.
They didn't bother.
Bother checking in.
They didn't see her.
They didn't see her sadness.
They could only see her,
For what she could do.
They could only see her,
For how she benefited them.
They couldn't see her broken heart.
They didn't bother checking in.
They wouldn't understand.
Understand her anger.
They wouldn't comprehend.
Comprehend her grief.
They wouldn't nurture her.
They would only scold her.
They didn't hold her,
How she needed to be held.
They didn't stay to wipe her tears.
They all just got up to leave,
Because it was all about them.
They would only support her,
To get something for them.
They would expect payback.
Payback is for them.
They wouldn't see her,
For who she really was.

They only saw her,
For what she could do.
She did so much.
So much for them.
She would stay for them,
And wipe their tears.
She would listen to them,
For hours and hours.
She would give all of her love.
Because that is who she is.
She loves and loves,
And expects nothing in return.
But once she started loving herself,
They all left.
Because what is in it for them?
*"She doesn't meet our needs.*
*Not anymore.*
*She changed.*
*We don't like this new girl.*
*She sees us for who we really are.*
*She sees our true colors.*
*Our true colors came out.*
*She doesn't see what she wants to see...*
*Not anymore.*
*She sees reality.*
*She doesn't see us with that illusion.*
*She no longer paints a picture.*
*A picture in her mind,*
*Of who we are.*
*Who we are to her...*
*She sees reality.*
*She sees what is real.*

*She understands clearly,*
*What we were doing to her.*
*She understands clearly,*
*That we were using her.*
*She understands clearly,*
*We were taking from her."*
They never saw her for who she really was.
Because all they cared about...
Was what was in it for them.
Self-centered,
And selfish.
Narcissistic and demeaning.
Belittling and silencing.
*"She needs to stay silent.*
*She needs to bow down.*
*Bow down to us.*
*Her needs don't matter.*
*Only ours do.*
*Punish her and belittle her.*
*That is what she is good for.*
*Her truth will be ignored.*
*Her voice will be silenced.*
*Her true self will be suppressed.*
*She will continue on,*
*Without any rest.*
*Because the only time she is worthy,*
*Is when she is doing.*
*When she is succeeding.*
*Don't talk,*
*Look pretty.*
*You are our object.*

*Our object for us.*
*Our object that we control.*
*Our object that we can ignore.*
*Pick up and put down,*
*Whenever we want.*
*But pick up our calls,*
*When we feel like calling.*
*Calling to pretend nothing is wrong.*
*Calling to say happy holidays,*
*And happy birthday.*
*Calling and texting to tell you what to do.*
*Calling to show...*
*Look,*
*We called you.*
*We picked up the phone,*
*We are putting in effort.*
*But this is only to manipulate you.*
*Manipulate and control.*
*This is what we do.*
*This is the disfunction.*
*This is how we treat you.*
*This is how we parent.*
*And you better accept this.*
*Play along and act like nothing is wrong.*
*You are our child,*
*And this is what we give you.*
*We give you this mistreatment,*
*Instead of giving you love.*
*We would rather abuse you,*
*Than to love you.*
*We would rather put you down,*

*Than to nurture you.*
*We would much rather have you accept.*
*Accept abuse.*
*Than to heal all of your wounds.*
*These wounds that we caused.*
*These wounds we like to reopen.*
*These wounds that we have,*
*That we pass down to you.*
*We would rather you stay.*
*Stay in your wounds.*
*Stay unhealed,*
*Because this is how we connect with you.*
*Don't get help.*
*Stay the same.*
*Stay like us...*
*We like you better this way.*
*The way you were.*
*The way you used to be.*
*The way you were,*
*When you took our shit.*
*When you took our abuse,*
*And never spoke up.*
*When you accepted our breadcrumbs.*
*These breadcrumbs you survived on.*
*We liked you better when you gave us everything.*
*Everything you had,*
*And left nothing for yourself.*
*Because it was easier for us,*
*To put you down.*
*It was easier for us,*
*To feel good.*

*We walked around feeling good.*
*Good about ourselves,*
*Because you were kicked down.*
*Kicked down by us.*
*You were kicked down,*
*While you held us up.*
*You were kicked down,*
*While giving us love.*
*You were kicked down,*
*But we stayed up on our pedestal.*
*You were kicked down.*
*We liked you down there.*
*We liked it,*
*So that we could look down on you.*
*We liked it,*
*So we could pretend we were better than you.*
*We liked it so much,*
*Until you stood up.*
*You stood up for yourself.*
*Until you stayed up,*
*While healing all of your wounds.*
*You stayed up and saw.*
*This illusion, we made.*
*This illusion, we created.*
*This illusion, we live in.*
*You left this illusion.*
*You left it for good.*
*You left us.*
*You left our abuse.*
*You left our game.*
*This cage we made...*

*We made it for you.*
*You left what you knew.*
*Everything you knew.*
*You did it for you...*
*How could you?"*

## Some Say…

Some say,
Suck it up.
Some say,
You have to let it go.
Some say,
Move on,
Some say,
It's time to be an adult.
Some say,
Shove it under the rug.
Some say,
Don't show yourself.
Some say,
Stay small.
Some say,
…But they are your parents,
Just let it go.
Some say,
Just stay.
Time is running out.
Some say,
Life is fragile.
Life is short.
Some say…
But what do I say?
Does it even matter,
What I say?
That I have say…
A say in my own life.
A say in how I am living my own life.

Some say,
Let everything stay the same.
Just as it is,
As it is right now.
Because it is easier.
Easier for who?
Easier for them?
The ones,
Who are doing the hurting.
The ones,
Doing the blaming.
The ones,
Doing the name calling.
The ones,
Giving silent treatment.
The ones,
Who give punishments.
The ones,
Who are in control.
Easier for who?
Easier for them?
Guess what?
Things change.
Things are not meant,
To stay the same.
Generational trauma.
Generational pain.
Passed down and passed down.
From them to me.
"This is the way.
The way it needs to be."
Well guess what?

It is not anymore.
Because things have changed.
My voice has been silenced.
Silenced my whole life.
My truth has been denied.
Denied my whole life.
My person.
My true self,
Has been shoved down.
Shoved down and walked on.
Punished and abused.
Scolded and belittled.
But not anymore.
I hold my power now.
My power is me.
My power,
I am holding.
Holding in my hands.
My worth can't be destroyed.
Destroyed by another man.
Another parent.
Another person.
Another human being.
Ever again.
My worth.
My power.
My love.
I hold these in my hands.
I will hold them so tightly,
And never let them go.
As I walk on my path,
And I move forward.

I take note that these are all that I need,
On my path.
I will take these,
As I let everything else go.
I will do what is best for me,
As I change these generational ways.
This trauma.
Passed down,
From generation to generation.
This trauma is not mine.
I will not carry it.
Starting fresh.
Starting new.
Teaching myself.
Staying true.
True to myself.
Standing my ground,
Instead of losing myself.
Losing myself to generational trauma.
Losing myself to please everyone else.
Losing myself,
Just to be loved.
Abandoning my soul,
Is what I was taught.
Taught from the beginning.
Taught from the start.
Taught that I don't matter,
But everyone else does.
I was taught to shove myself down.
I was taught to take everyone's shit.
I was taught to make myself small.
These are the teachings.

The teachings I learned.
These are the ways,
That I am putting away.
Putting away.
Putting them down,
Releasing them.
Re-teaching myself.
I matter.
I always have.
I have a voice.
I will share my truth.
I will stand up for myself,
And give it back to you.
I am important.
I will not be ignored.
I will not be walked on,
Not anymore.
I will hold my breath,
As I take this leap.
As I take this step,
Away from my life.
My life that I knew.
Everything I knew.
Everything I was.
Everything is gone,
I will become,
Who I was always meant to be.
I will do this,
As I set myself free.

## Your Own Arms.

Isn't it sad...
Sad that you abandoned yourself?
Isn't it sad...
That you couldn't be yourself?
Isn't it sad...
That you stunted who you were?
Just to belong.
Just to be part of something.
Just to say that you are loved.
Loved by them.
Just to be wrapped up in arms.
Arms that would betray you.
Held by arms.
Arms that would throw you away.
Throw you away,
Like you were nothing.
Throw you away,
Like you didn't matter.
Arms that held you.
Held you when you were bleeding.
Held you when you were down.
Arms that wanted you to stay like that.
Stay kicked down.
Stay bleeding.
Stay for them.
Arms that held you.
Held you down.
Arms that would control you.
Control your every move.
Arms that were there.

There to hold you in your place.
Arms that had other motives.
Motives for them.
Go out and do for them,
You owe them that.
You owe them because,
That is what you do.
You owe them.
You owe them because they held you.
They held you when you were down.
You owe them just because...
Just because you are their kid.
They were the arms,
The arms you knew.
Arms that expected.
Expected something in return.
These arms that held you,
Would one day destroy you.
These arms that held you,
Would one day betray you.
How do you trust?
Trust to be held?
Held by other arms.
Held just because.
Just because you are you.
No one has ever showed this to you.
Showed you how it was supposed to be.
Just to be held.
Held and loved.
Just because.
Just because you are you.
Just because you are important.

Just because you matter.
Just because.
No one showed you what it would be like.
What it would be like,
To be held unconditionally.
No conditions.
Just to be held.
No one showed you this.
The arms that you run to,
Are not the arms.
Those are not the arms,
You should be running to.
The only arms you ever knew,
Those are the arms you have to walk away from.
Walk away,
From those arms.
Those are the arms.
The only arms you knew.
But those are the arms,
That were supposed to keep you safe.
And those were the very arms,
That did not keep you safe.
Those are the arms,
That held you for their own gain.
Those are the arms,
That caused you so much pain.
Those are the arms,
That held you.
But they didn't really hold you.
They kept you controlled,
And they used you.
They kept you on a leash.

This leash of control.
These are the arms.
The only arms you knew.
They didn't hold you with their love.
They didn't hold you with their heart.
They threw you away.
Those arms you knew.
Those arms you kept running to,
Just to be thrown away.
Those arms you would run to,
Just to feel safe.
Those arms you would run to,
And you had to join in on the game.
Put your mask on,
To join the façade.
This façade they put on.
Put on for the world.
Those arms you would run to,
Because where else would you go?
Once you found safety in your own body,
You no longer needed to run into those arms.
Once you found safety inside of yourself...
You became the arms that you always needed.
You became that embrace that made you feel safe.
You became the arms that would never let you go.
You became the arms that you needed so badly.
You held yourself finally,
With your own arms.
You held yourself finally,
With all of your own love.
You held yourself finally,
In your own arms.

That was the day you stopped running,
To everyone else.

## They Can't See

They can't see…
Can't see where I am.
They can't see…
Because they don't know loss.
They don't know betrayal.
They don't know grief.
They cannot see.
They just can't see me.
They can't understand.
They just can't see.
They don't grasp that I had to let go…
Let go of parts of me.
Parts of me that they knew.
They don't understand.
I had to let go of my own hand.
I had to let go…
So many times.
I know this process.
I know it well.
Because I know what loss feels like.
I know what it takes.
I have to say goodbye.
Goodbye to them.
But then I have to say goodbye,
To me.
The parts of myself that had love for them.
The parts of myself that held onto them.
The parts of me that held their hand.
Those parts of me,
I had to grieve.

I had to say goodbye to those parts.
Those parts of me that they knew.
That is what they can't see.
They can't see it.
They can't see this process.
I can't even describe.
I cannot describe how painful it is.
I cannot describe how awful it is.
How awful it is to detach from myself.
I cannot even describe the pain I feel,
Each time I let go.
Each time I say goodbye.
It is a sadness.
This deep sadness.
This sadness buried so deep down.
This sadness I feel,
And carry it around.
I am mourning the losses.
I am mourning myself.
This grief I carry,
That no one can see.
This grief I know well.
It is so deep in me.
This loss I carry.
I carry it close.
Close to my heart,
Because it used to be love.
Love that I had.
Love that I gave.
Love that I felt,
Straight from my heart.
This love has transformed.

Transformed into grief.
This grief that I carry...
I carry with me.

## Just Be.

Just be.
Just be free.
Today I am focused on just being me.
Today I am focused on my peace I feel.
Today I am focused on the me that I am.
Nowhere to go.
Nowhere to be.
Nothing to do.
Nothing to achieve.
Today just is.
It just is.
Today I just am.
I am just me.
Today I get to be.
I get to just be.
I am focused on this...
Just be free.
Just be at peace.
Just be.
Just be.
Just be me.
Nothing to prove.
Nowhere to go.
Not a thing to do.
Breathe in.
Breathe out.
That is it.
My breath.
My heart.
My soul.

My peace.
This is it.
Just be.

## Choosing Myself...Over Everything Else

If I shared my feelings.
If I used my voice.
If I became me.
If I opened up.
If I spoke the truth.
If I pointed something out.
If I raised my voice.
If I went against the control...
I would be punished.
I would be left.
I would be dismissed,
Or I would be yelled at.
I would be scolded.
I would be shut down.
I was never right...
Or listened to.
I wasn't allowed.
Allowed to be myself.
I wasn't allowed to just be,
How I wanted to be.
I wasn't allowed,
To do what I wanted.
I was not asked...
I was told.
Told what to do.
Told to be a certain way.
Told to be this way or else.
This black or white.
This way or that way.
Be this or be that.

---

But do not be what you want.
Do not be how you really are.
Shove down your true self.
Abandon yourself always...
Always for us.
When I do what I want now,
I feel this fear.
When I become who I really am,
I feel this fear.
When I say what I want to say,
I feel this fear.
Constantly waiting for the other shoe to drop.
I have this fear...
This fear of punishment.
This fear I will be blamed.
This fear of what will happen.
This fear of being left.
This fear of being punished,
When I show my true self.
My whole self,
With every emotion.
Who I really am.
Showing myself.
I suppressed who I was.
I suppressed my true self.
I abandoned myself,
Just so that I would be loved.
I abandoned myself,
Just so that I would be seen.
I abandoned myself,
Just so that I would fit in.
Because every time I revealed myself,

I would be punished.
Blamed.
Scolded.
Or left.
Every time I revealed myself,
I would turn into their project.
Someone trying to fix me.
Someone trying to pity me.
Projecting their wounds,
Onto me.
Projecting their scars.
Projecting their hurt.
Projecting anything,
So that they could just feel good.
I would take it and take it.
I would grab it and hold it.
I would make myself small,
So they would feel big.
I would give them what they want,
And abandon myself.
Each and every time.
I abandoned myself,
And thought that was who I was.
I abandoned myself,
To be around everyone else.
Doing what they wanted.
Doing what they loved.
Appeasing them,
While leaving myself behind.
Loving them,
While I left myself unloved.
Doing and going...

Choosing everyone else.
Choosing them over myself.
Choosing them over me.
Making choices,
Over-giving my empathy.
Giving and giving,
Until I had nothing left.
It is my turn now.
Time to choose myself.
Choosing for me,
Over everyone else.
Choosing me.
Choosing what I love.
Moving away,
From everyone else.
Moving away,
From what doesn't feel right.
Moving away,
From what is not for me.
Moving away,
From what is not safe.
Choosing for me.
Choosing for myself.
Firmly believing.
Believing in myself.
Firmly loving.
Loving who I am.
Firmly receiving.
Receiving from myself.
Firmly accepting.
Accepting the past.
Firmly forgiving.

Forgiving who I was.
Firmly moving on.
Moving on from my pain.
Firmly living.
Living for this moment.
Firmly being.
Just be in this peace.
Firmly breathing.
Breathe in.
Breathe out.
Feel this safety.
Feel this peace.
Feel this moment.
Feel this now.
Connecting with myself.
Connecting with my body.
Connecting with my heart.
Connecting with my soul.
Connecting with my love.
Connecting with God.
Connecting with nature.
Connecting with choices.
The choices I will make.
These choices I make,
I make them for myself.
Choosing myself,
Over everything else.

# Awakened

Not speaking up.
Hold it in.
Keep it all inside.
Suppress it all.
You are not worthy.
Worthy to speak.
You are not important...
Important enough.
This is what you were taught.
This is what you will release.
Your voice matters.
So do your beliefs.
Your truth matters.
You are not holding it in.
Not anymore.
You have found your people.
The people that make you feel safe.
You have trust in yourself.
You have moved away from disfunction.
You have left the chaos.
You no longer have to fear.
Fear their reactions.
You no longer have to hide.
Hide your true self.
You no longer have to abandon.
Abandon who you are.
You no longer will be blamed,
When you have done nothing wrong.
You no longer will be punished,
When you stand up for yourself.

You no longer will be dismissed.
Dismissed when you speak up.
You no longer will be left,
When there is conflict.
You have left what you know.
Everything you know.
You have left what dimmed your light.
You have found love for yourself.
You now know how it feels,
When you don't choose yourself.
You abandoned yourself,
For everyone else.
You abandoned your love,
To give it all out.
You acted out,
So that you would be seen.
You went off on your own,
Just to feel peace.
You overdid,
Just to avoid and achieve.
You didn't pay attention.
Pay attention to the signs.
The signs your body was telling you.
Telling you the whole time.
Sending out pain.
Sending out discomfort.
Sending out problems.
Problems that you felt.
Felt in your body.
Your body would tell you.
Tell you every time.
Your body was speaking.

---

Your body spoke.
Your body yelled,
Until you awoke.
You have awakened.
Awakened to your soul.
You have awakened.
Awakened to the pain.
You have awakened.
Awakened to your heart.
You have awakened.
Awakened to your voice.
You have awakened.
Awakened to the truth.
You have become awakened.
Awakened to you.
You have returned home,
And found who you really are.

# This Road I Am On

My support system gone.
My support system that I relied on.
My support.
My love.
Who do I trust now?
Who do I go to?
Where do I belong?
...now that everything is gone.
No one can see,
What happened to me.
No one can see,
This pain in my heart.
No one can see,
Because I wear it so well.
I wear my pain well.
I don't show it at all.
I don't show it.
I hide it,
Because who would I trust.
The last time I trusted,
And showed myself...
I was betrayed.
The last time I showed my pain,
They all turned on me.
The last time I showed my pain,
They all ran away.
People don't stay.
People run away.
The people I knew.
The people I loved.

The people I wrapped my arms around.
The people I inserted into my heart.
The people I was connected to.
The people I held.
The people I would have done anything for.
Those people...
My people...
Those people betrayed me.
They broke my heart.
*It is important to find,*
*That love in yourself.*
*It is important to accept.*
*Accept this is your lane.*
*The lane you are in,*
*Is the lane people don't want.*
*They don't want to join you,*
*In this lane you have picked.*
*They don't want to see,*
*The things that you see.*
*They don't want to look at,*
*The things you point out.*
*They don't want to embrace you,*
*As you change.*
*Because as you change,*
*It is uncomfortable for them.*
*As you change,*
*You mirror it all back to them.*
*All of what you are letting go of,*
*It is all being mirrored back to them.*
*Things they don't want to feel.*
*Things they don't want to see.*
*Things they want to push down.*

*Things they want to go away.*
*You are mirroring back to them,*
*A reality they don't want to know.*
*They don't want to go down this road.*
*This road that you chose.*
*This lane you are in,*
*Is yours alone.*
*You will walk it alone,*
*As you leave people behind.*
*You will walk it alone,*
*As you pick up to find.*
*Tools you will need,*
*To make it through this lane.*
*This lane, you have chosen.*
*You have chosen for yourself.*
*You cannot have expectations for anyone else.*
*You cannot expect them to join you in this lane.*
*This lane you are in,*
*Is the most difficult lane.*
*This lane you are in...*
*Many won't come.*
*They will not come with you.*
*You have to leave them.*
*You must keep going.*
*You must not stop.*
*You must not give up.*
*You have made it this far.*
*It is time to keep moving.*
*Let go once again.*
*You know this by now.*
*You must keep letting go,*
*In this lane that you chose.*

---

*The lane you are in,*
*Is not paved well.*
*The lane you are in...*
*Many won't follow.*
*It is important to know this,*
*As you move forward.*
*The lane you are in,*
*Is filled with grief.*
*The lane you are in,*
*Is filled with pain.*
*Pain you must feel,*
*To take a step.*
*Just one step forward,*
*You must feel this pain.*
*To take another step,*
*Means more and more pain.*
*More than the last.*
*Just three steps,*
*Feels like you are dead.*
*This is the lane.*
*The lane you are in.*
*No one knows this road.*
*This road you are on.*
*No one can see,*
*The burdens you carry.*
*No one can see,*
*How hard it really is.*
*No one can see,*
*Because their road is not like this.*
*Their road is easier.*
*Their road is known.*
*Their road is familiar.*

*Their road is fun.*
*They don't have to navigate.*
*Navigate at all.*
*Because their road has been cleared.*
*Cleared for them.*
*Cleared by their parents.*
*Cleared by their husbands.*
*Cleared by nurturing loved ones,*
*Taking care of them.*
*Cleared by love.*
*They know love.*
*They follow their families love,*
*Down their family road.*
*They follow their path,*
*That was given to them.*
*Paved and cleared.*
*Cleared for them.*
*Surrounded by support,*
*Waiting for them.*
*Even when they choose to pave a new road,*
*They have their support system.*
*Their support system comes.*
*Their support system lined up,*
*Cheering them on.*
*Their new road,*
*They still have their support.*
*Their new road they pave,*
*Their families come.*
*Their families come along,*
*Because that is what love is.*
*Love is support.*
*Love just is.*

---

*Love is not taken away.*
*Love is not conditional.*
*Love is not transactional.*
*Love is not a cage.*
*You have left a road,*
*That was paved for you.*
*This road that left you,*
 *With wounds and sorrow.*
*This road that left you,*
*Feeling unimportant.*
*This road that left you,*
*Feeling small.*
*This road that left you,*
*With your voice shoved down.*
*This road that kept you,*
*From your intuition.*
*This road that kept you,*
*From your heart.*
*This road that kept you,*
*From your soul.*
*This road that left you,*
*Sacrificing yourself.*
*You must find a new road.*
*Because that road was not yours.*
*It never was.*
*Your road has been chosen.*
*Chosen for you.*
*Chosen by God,*
*Handed down to you.*
*Your road is hard.*
*Your road has not been cleared.*
*You are clearing as you go,*

*On this much slower road.*
*You are learning as you go,*
*As you push through the pain.*
*This pain that was avoided,*
*From generations before.*
*This generational trauma,*
*Has been carried all this time.*
*This generational trauma,*
*Has been passed down to you.*
*This generational trauma,*
*You are finally putting down.*
*You are putting it all down,*
*Because it was never yours.*
This pain that I am feeling,
It is not even mine.
This risk that I am taking,
I am doing it for me.
I am finally putting myself first.
I am finally learning what love really is.
Love has been blocked,
By carrying this pain.
Love has been turned off,
All this time.
Love has not existed,
Because of this pain.
This pain.
This trauma,
Has been in the way.
I am putting it all down,
It is time for me to be brave.
For generations and generations,
They keep passing it down.

For generations and generations,
I will be the last.
I will be the last to hold this pain in my hands.
I will be the last,
As I allow this pain in.
As I allow this pain to flow throughout me.
My body is my vessel,
To let this pain in.
Let this pain in.
Let this pain out.
Let it all flow.
Flow throughout me,
Let it all move.
Move completely out of me.
My body is my vessel,
That no one can see.
They cannot see this process.
This process in me.
No one can see.
No one but me.
I see it.
I feel it.
Then I let it go.
Never again will I know,
This pain I am letting go.
This is what keeps me…
Keeps me alive.
This is what keeps me…
Keeps me to survive.
Survive this process.
Survive this pain.
Keep on surviving.

Keep on going.
Making a difference.
Making an impact.
Handing out love,
To everyone else.
Unconditional love.
First to myself,
Then to the world.
Spreading it out,
From me to them.
Spreading this love...
This love to the world.
As I let go of this generational curse.
This curse.
This pain.
This misery.
This sorrow.
As I let it all go,
I feel the love.
This love has been within me,
All this time.
This love I didn't know existed,
Because it was covered in pain.
Pain that was mine,
And pain that was not.
I carried my own pain,
Along with generations and generations.
I am finally letting it go,
As I create this new road.
Standing all by myself,
Out on my own.
Continuing on.

Not giving up.
Navigating this road.
This road I am on.

## ...Along With Her Worth

She carried so much pain.
She carried it well.
She carried it around with a smile on her face.
She carried her pain.
She carried it with her,
She held it and felt it,
As she acknowledged it all.
She sat with her pain.
She sat in silence.
She carried this betrayal.
It was time to feel it.
It was time to see it.
It was time to hear it.
She decided it was time.
Time to hold it.
She finally understands.
Understands herself.
Understands her pain,
Because she stopped shoving it down.
She finally stopped,
Abandoning herself.
She finally stopped sacrificing herself.
She finally stood up.
Stood up for herself.
It was finally time,
To become who she really was.
It was finally time,
To face her emotions,
Each and every emotion.
It was time,

To face her grief.
Her grief.
Her loss.
She carried it around.
She carried it with her,
Each and everyday.
She carried this with her,
Deeply in her heart.
She carried this with her,
As she took a step forward.
She took steps forward,
As she cried her tears.
So many tears,
Flowing from her eyes.
So much grief,
Filled her soul.
So much pain.
Pain inside.
She took steps forward,
Holding her heart.
Her heart in her hands,
Along with her worth.

## Love, Just Love.

This root of betrayal.
This root I will get.
The root of it all,
Is "I was not important enough."
It was my responsibility.
It was my job.
It was put on me.
It was my job to fix.
It was my punishment.
I was to blame.
I must play their game.
If I choose to walk away.
It is me choosing myself.
But each time I choose myself,
I would get love taken away.
I was taught self-sacrifice,
Do as you are told.
Do not do what you want.
Do not follow your heart.
You stand by us.
You cower down.
Do not take care of yourself.
Make yourself small.
Swallow your truth,
Each and every time.
Do not be yourself.
We will not have your back.
Only if you do for us.
Only if you do this.
Only if you behave.

Only if you do not speak up.
Only if you are good.
Only if you do as you are told.
Only if we have control.
Only if you are happy.
Only if it's convenient for us.
Only if...
Because we have taught you transactional love.
The root of this betrayal.
The root is transactional love.
This root,
I will release.
I have learned unconditional love.
Love myself,
No matter what.
Love myself,
Through it all.
Love is the answer.
Love without conditions.
Love without transactions.
Love without punishments.
Love without blame.
Love without the pain.
Love,
Just love.
Unconditional love.

## ...It Will All Make Sense

This path.
This path she is on.
This path, all alone.
She travels down.
This path not chosen,
By her family members and friends.
This path is hers.
And hers alone.
This path of pain.
This path of grief.
This path of her choosing herself,
As she walks away.
Walks away from abuse.
Walks away from what reopens her wounds.
Walks away from,
Silent treatment and punishment.
Breadcrumbs of love.
Blame and dismissal.
Control and insecurity.
Taking everything personally.
Taking love away from her,
When she misbehaves.
They will label her bad...
"...Here she goes again."
Having these expectations of her.
Projecting their emotions,
Making her the scapegoat.
Using her to fulfil their needs.
Not seeing her properly,
As they live in survival mode.

Go.
Go.
Go.
Get everything done.
Check off a box.
They just want to have fun.
Everything happy.
Everything is good.
Using her to distract.
Distract and avoid.
Avoidance is what they know.
They want her to join.
Join in on this.
Join in on avoidance.
As they only acknowledge.
Acknowledge the good,
And only the good.
Acknowledge her,
Only when they get something back.
Back from her,
This is what she is good for.
Giving and giving...
Giving it all.
Giving and giving...
Giving her heart.
Giving and giving...
While she accepts breadcrumbs.
Breadcrumbs of love,
Is all that she knew.
Living in denial.
Living in an illusion.
An illusion she'll walk away from.

She'll walk away from this illusion.
Walking right into reality,
As she walks away from everything she knew.
Walking right into emotions.
Emotions she was not equipped to feel.
Finding her love.
Finding her light.
Finding her worth,
As she walks away.
Walks away from everything dimming her light.
Holding her worth.
Her worth in her hands.
Listening to her intuition,
As she walks ahead.
Opening her heart,
As she feels her pain.
Keeping her heart open,
As she feels the grief.
Finding safety,
And staying there.
Calming her nervous system,
As she learns to repair.
Repair her wounds.
Repair her heart.
Repair and mend,
As she walks this road.
This road not traveled,
By anyone else.
This road.
This path.
This journey through the dark.
It will all be worth it.

Worth it in the end.
The end of this road,
It will all make sense.
The end of this road,
Brings her right to her love and light.

## It Is Time To Put The Sugar Down

Ruffling feathers.
Rocking the boat.
Crushing the illusion.
Speaking the truth.
Upsetting them.
Making them mad.
"It is all her fault…
Why is she so bad."
She is done accepting this abuse.
Leaving the cage.
Putting an end to this game.
Taking this fear,
And blowing it away.
Kissing it goodbye,
Walking into a new lane,
A new lane of self-love.
A new lane of bravery.
A new lane that is hers.
A new lane that feels lonely,
Because it is so new.
All new.
It is new.
Nothing is the same.
Everything is different.
Nothing feels the same.
Nothing is familiar.
Nothing feels comfortable.
Leaving the old.
Embracing the new.
Feeling the grief.

---

Accepting the past.
Feeling the pain.
Speaking assertively.
Choosing differently.
Making amends.
Amends with the events.
The events that happened.
The events that shaped her.
Learning the lessons.
Finding forgiveness.
Collecting the tools.
Having compassion.
Understanding and acceptance,
As she becomes awakened.
Consciousness is radiating.
Radiating out of her.
Her aura has changed,
As she chose a new way.
Making space,
As she finds freedom.
She found her freedom,
As she found her love.
She found her peace,
Inside of her love.
She knew just who she was,
As she found her light.
Her light was being hidden.
Hidden by darkness.
She had to walk right in.
Right into the darkness.
Right into the pain.
Right into emotions.

Right into the grief,
That was dimming her light.
She walked right in.
Right into her demons.
She listened closely.
She gave them the attention.
The attention they needed.
They needed to be heard.
They needed to be seen.
They needed to be felt.
Walking right into,
These demons she kept.
She held them and loved them.
Each one of them,
She acknowledged.
Every single demon,
Was nurtured and spoiled.
Spoiled in silence,
As she walked away from the noise.
The noise that kept her.
Kept her from them.
The noise that kept her demons inside.
The noise that distracted,
Her from herself.
The noise was her distraction.
This noise was her addiction.
This noise was her avoidance.
Running from her demons.
Running from her pain.
Running so fast,
She could barely breathe.
Barely breathing.

Barely surviving.
Running from her pain.
Her pain she covered up.
She covered it up,
To love everyone else.
She covered it up.
As she over gave.
She covered it all up…
All of her pain.
She put everyone else,
Before herself.
She pleased everyone else,
While she covered up her pain.
She sacrificed her whole being,
Because that is what she knew.
She knew it so well.
That is what she was taught.
She knew she needed to put herself first.
This would feel different,
Because this not what she knew.
This would feel selfish.
Dynamics would change.
Her voice would become different.
Her words would become real.
Real and truthful.
Assertive and honest.
Blunt without the sugar.
Sugar coating and pleasing,
Is all that she knew.
Time to put the sugar down…
It was time for the truth.
Her truth comes out.

Her needs would change,
So would her standards.
Standing up for herself,
Finally.
This is what she deserves.
She deserved this from day one,
But was not ever shown.
She deserved the very best.
She deserved this from day one.
She deserved the love she gave out.
She deserved this love she gave away.
She deserved this from herself,
But she was constantly looking away.
Looking around,
At everyone else.
*What does everyone else need?*
*Who do I need to be...*
*So they will feel pleased.*
Pleased and happy....
She served this all day.
She served this on a silver platter,
That she was just giving away.
Giving to everyone else,
While leaving herself empty.
Giving and giving,
Until there was nothing left.
Nothing was left...
This was her time.
Her time to shine...
She needed to face this loneliness.
This loneliness was her.
Her little girl.

---

Starving for attention.
Attention from her.
Attention she was giving away...
While abandoning herself.
She didn't even know,
There was any other way.
She never believed,
That she deserved this love.
She couldn't see her light,
Because she was constantly looking away.
She never believed in herself,
Until now.
She now believes in herself,
Wholeheartedly.
She believes it.
She trusts it.
She believes in herself.
She believes in her own love.
She will choose.
Choose for herself.
She will choose her life now...
It is finally her turn.
Her turn is NOW.

## All Times

I have this resilience.
This resilience in me.
Radiating resilience.
Taking it all on.
Being strong,
While not falling down.
No one to hold me.
Hold me up.
No one to support me.
*Keep going and going.*
*Keep moving and doing.*
*Rest is not important...*
*Avoidance is the way.*
*Put a smile on my face.*
*Put the pain away.*
Those were my old ways.
I found new ways.
I found myself.
Silence and serenity.
Breathe in.
Breathe out.
Rest and feel.
Hold myself up.
Stay up and heal.
Heal my wounds.
No one is coming to save me.
It is me.
That someone is me.
Manipulation brought me down.
Dimmed my light.

I went to the darkness.
Just for a minute.
Uncovered my light.
It was there the whole time.
I found my love in my light.
My freedom and my peace.
Forgiveness and acceptance.
Courage and safety.
These were in me.
I just needed to believe.
Never again will I allow,
My light to be dimmed.
Walking away from control.
Never again walking on eggshells.
Fulfilling their needs,
While they use me.
Over and over.
I allowed this to go on,
For far too long.
I put a stop to it now...
It is not going on anymore.
I was not taught.
I was not shown.
Shown how to love.
I was given breadcrumbs.
Breadcrumbs to survive.
My whole life,
I survived on these breadcrumbs.
My whole life,
I put myself aside.
Not anymore
I choose differently this time.

Make a new choice.
This time,
For me.
This time...
& all times.

# Dear Dad

Instead of being sorry.
Instead of being accountable.
Instead of protecting me.
Instead of keeping me safe.
Instead of loving me,
The way a father should have.
The way that I needed.
You chose yourself,
And taught me self-sacrifice.
Instead of teaching me,
To love myself.
Instead of teaching me,
To stand up for myself.
You taught me blame and punishment.
You taught me I was unimportant.
You betrayed me.
You left me.
You chose yourself.
This is just how I felt.
I was blinded,
My whole life.
I was blinded,
Because I loved you.
You were my dad...
The one I looked up to.
The one I saw as protection.
The one I looked up to for safety.
The one who I called for everything.
You were the one,
I would have done anything for.

You were the one,
I cared for.
You were the one,
I held up on a pedestal.
You were my hero.
You were my star.
You were the one,
I had in my heart.
And you were also the one,
Who allowed abuse to go on.
You were the one,
Who allowed me to be punished.
Punished instead of loved.
You were the one,
Who allowed mistreatment.
You were the one,
Who shut my voice down.
You were the one,
Who didn't stand up for me.
You were the one,
Who blamed me.
You were the one,
Who allowed those knives to be thrown.
You were the one,
Who ultimately broke my heart.
Betrayed me in the end...
Even though you knew it was wrong.
Let time go by...
Then expected me to shove it all under the rug.
Wanted me,
To join back in the game.

Wanted me,
To return to that cage.
That cage of control.
That cage I was in...
I was in for too long...
I couldn't go back...
I had to leave.
You wanted me,
To abandon myself.
Self-sacrifice myself...
Once again.
Over and over I did that...
I did it my whole life...
I can't do it anymore.
I love you so much.
I still do.
I can't be there for you now,
Because I had to choose myself.
I must choose me,
And walk away from that cage.
That cage I was in...
I was in for too long.
Not being treated the way,
I deserved to be treated.
Not being loved the way,
I deserved to be loved.
Not being heard the way,
I deserved to be heard.
You wouldn't see me,
The way I needed to be seen.
Because you were too busy closing your eyes,

Choosing for yourself.
Choosing what lit you up…
Pretending nothing was wrong.
I was always cowering down,
Because I was afraid.
I was afraid of you,
Because you failed to keep me safe.
I pretended to be,
A person I wasn't.
I became someone else,
Just so I could be your daughter.
I wore my mask,
Just to keep you happy.
I joined in on the façade,
Just to stand by your side.
I wore my mask for your love…
Just to be loved.
Loved by you.
I took my mask off…
I can't do it anymore.
I need to be me,
The me I deserve.
I deserve to be,
Who I was always meant to be.
I need to be me,
And leave that insanity.
I couldn't see it until now…
Now that it is too late.
Too late to tell you this…
Because it is too late for you to see,
For you to understand.

It is too late for us,
To mend and repair.
It is too late for me to teach you this.
This was never my job,
To teach you things.
Maybe if you were open to hear,
But you closed me off.
You pushed me away,
One final time.
You said things to me,
That a father should never say.
Just for you to feel big...
For you to feel good.
I can't do it anymore.
I must move away from all of this.
Walk away from this.
Walk away from old ways.
Walk away from that cage.
Old ways that you know...
You only know those ways.
And you are not open to learn.
You are not open to hear.
Because it is too late for all that.
You will forget it all...
So ironic.
The memories will fade.
You have now fallen under the spell,
Of a smear campaign.
Trashing my name,
Instead of admitting your faults.
It is too late for us.

To learn conflict and repair,
Because you made a choice.
You made it for you.
You chose yourself.
You always did.
Never putting yourself aside,
For any of your kids.
But you do it all the time.
Every time for your wife.
You made this choice.
You did it for you.
I must do this.
I must do it for me.
Walking away,
To leave you over there.
Sending you love.
Because no matter what...
No matter the storms.
No matter your words.
They were not right.
Words a father should not say.
Say to his daughter.
Put her down.
Put the blame on me.
I took the blame my whole life.
I did this for you...
I did this because I love you.
I loved you then.
I love you still.
I love you now.
I always will.
Sending you love.

On this day.
My heart was broken.
Broken by you.
But it still has love.
Love for you.

## It Was All In My Heart.

Seeing myself.
Loving myself.
Hearing myself.
Understanding myself.
Every single part.
This is me.
Walking out of denial...
Into the truth.
Right into reality.
Oh wow...
It is hitting me.
It makes sense to me now.
It all makes sense.
It was all a lesson.
It was all a teacher.
Everything I needed.
To uncover.
Uncover my wounds.
Uncover my pain.
Understand myself,
And cry my tears.
Nurture myself.
Give myself love.
Learn to accept,
And forgive it all.
It finally makes sense.
All of it.
My clarity,
Came to me.
Came to me,

Inside the darkest parts.
The darkest parts,
I did not want to see.
I stopped self-sacrifice.
I started to love it all.
Love every single part,
As I let myself fall.
Fall into the lowest.
The darkest moments.
Fall into the hardest.
Hardest feelings.
Fall into the longest.
The longest nights.
Fall into the loneliest,
Part of my life.
Let the loneliness in.
Let in the fear.
Let the anger arise.
Let the tears stream down,
Straight from my eyes.
Feel my heart break.
Feel the crack in my heart.
Feel the betrayal and abandonment,
And then let it go.
Let it all go.
Set myself free.
I am holding my freedom.
Inside of my peace.
I am standing here on the earth.
Feeling the dirt in my toes.
Reflecting on it all,
As I stand tall.

As I became this wildflower.
As I grew threw it all.
Grew through the storms,
Grew through the haze.
Grew through the hurricanes.
Every single one,
That came my way.
This wildflower that I am,
Bloomed through it all.
My roots became grounded.
Grounded in myself.
Grounded in my faith.
Grounded in my heart.
This wildflower that I am.
That I was from the start.
From the beginning.
The very beginning.
It was all in my heart.

# Sometimes They Loved Her

Sometimes they loved her.
Sometimes they didn't.
Sometimes they rewarded her.
Sometimes they punished her.
She didn't know what to expect.
She didn't know any other way.
*"Always be perfect.*
*Don't make a mistake.*
*Assumptions and expectations."*
Everything went their way.
She went with the flow.
She didn't speak up.
*"Don't rock the boat.*
*Don't do anything wrong.*
*Do for us,*
*Always do for us."*
This is what she knew.
This is what she will undo.
Using her voice,
And speaking up.
Moving away when it doesn't feel right.
Just being herself,
Was never enough.
Just being herself,
She didn't feel loved.
She didn't feel taken care of.
Communication wasn't used.
Because it was just assumed.
Assumed she would play along.
Play along with the game.

The game they played,
Until she found a new way to walk.
She chose a new path.
This way was different.
Different than what they knew.
Different than what *she* knew.
She would go to the unknown.
Vulnerability and surrender,
Without the control.
Give everything up.
Let it all go.
Become who she wants.
Become who she was always supposed to be.
Leaving behind her mask,
And setting herself free.
Leaving behind,
Her old ways.
Leaving behind all that she knew.
Feel the pain,
As she becomes new.
She must not talk back.
Talk back to them,
She must follow the rules.
The rules,
They give.
She must do as she is told.
She must not use her voice,
Or things will be taken away.
Transactional love.
This is what she knew.
These transactions have stopped,
Now that she has love for herself.

---

Pretty words that mean nothing.
All that smooth talking.
Telling her everything she wants to hear.
Telling her words they don't mean,
Telling her words.
Words.
Words.
Words.
Words with no action.
When there was an action,
It came with an expectation.
Every action they gave her,
Came with an expectation.
Every action they gave her,
Did not come from their hearts.
The actions they gave her,
Came with a cost.
This cost of self-sacrifice.
She must love them.
More than herself.
She must pay them back.
She must do something for them too.
She must not be herself.
She must leave herself behind.
She must not speak her mind.
She must not have feelings.
The very minute she changes,
And starts loving herself.
The very moment she speaks up,
They take things away.
Turn their back and leave her,
Because this is what they do best.

The very minute she chooses herself,
Over everyone else.
This is when she is scolded.
This is when she is punished.
These repercussions will keep her small.
Keep her down.
Keep her from herself.
This transactional love...
She will leave this behind.
These wounds they left,
She will mend.
She will speak up now.
She will speak her mind.
She will choose herself.
Choose herself every single time.
She will choose herself.
She will not be silenced.
She will stop being controlled.
She will get off the leash.
She will stop meeting their every need.
She will learn to meet her own needs.
She will accept her past.
She will love unconditionally,
Without putting herself aside.
She will put herself first,
Each and every time.
She will rest when she needs it.
She will continue to look inside.
She will look deep inside,
And heal her wounds.
As she heals her wounds,
She becomes confident in leaving it all behind.

---

She will not look back.
She will not turn back.
She will forever be changed,
As she feels her pain.

## His Eyes

His eyes.
Those eyes.
His eyes were closed.
They opened for a second,
Just to see.
Just in time to see me fall.
This is the only time they saw me,
As I fell.
They saw me.
They saw me fall.
His arms,
Did not catch me...
As I fell.
His arms failed me,
Through it all.
His eyes failed to see me.
He just did not see me.
He looked the other way.
He walked the other way.
He chose himself,
Over me.
His eyes,
Did not see me.
They did not see me,
For who I really was.
His eyes were shut,
The entire time.
His eyes stayed closed,
When I needed him the most.
His eyes were on someone else,

As I fell.
His eyes were supposed to see me.
See my pain.
His arms were supposed to catch me,
If I fell.
His arms were around someone else,
While his eyes were shut.
He shut his eyes so he wouldn't see.
He wouldn't see this mask she wore.
He wouldn't see how my heart was torn.
He wouldn't see this game she played.
He wouldn't see me hide my pain.
He wouldn't see me cry my tears.
He wouldn't see me wipe them away.
He wouldn't see me put on a face.
A happy face.
A face with a smile.
A smile that was covering so much pain.
This mask I wore,
He wouldn't see.
He refused to see.
He wouldn't listen.
Listen to me.
He shut his eyes one final time.
He took his arms completely away.
He wouldn't look.
He wouldn't open his eyes.
He lived in his own illusion,
And refused to see.
He wouldn't see me,
Standing here.
He wouldn't see me,

Wipe my own tears.
He wouldn't see me,
Use my voice.
He wouldn't see me,
Self-sacrifice.
Sacrifice myself for him.
Abandon myself just to be seen.
Leave myself behind,
To be there for him.
He wouldn't see reality.
He would only see what was best for him.
He wouldn't see me standing here,
Holding myself up.
Drying my tears.
He wouldn't see me open my eyes.
My eyes would open,
And stare right at him.
They would stare right into his eyes.
His eyes that couldn't see me,
But I could see him.
His eyes would look the other way,
Just as I begged him to stay.
His eyes would look down,
Down at my feet.
His eyes would see my feet,
Walking away.
His mouth stayed shut,
As I left for good.
His eyes stayed shut,
As he let me walk.
His eyes wouldn't see any of this,
Because they stayed shut.

So he could feel good.
It was all about him.
It always was.
His eyes stayed shut,
As he passed out transactional love.
His eyes stayed shut,
As he played the game.
His eyes stayed shut,
As he tore me apart.
As he had these expectations of me.
His eyes stayed shut,
As he stayed in the façade.
His eyes stayed shut,
As I left for good.
This felt like I was unimportant to him.
Betrayed and left.
Unimportant and afraid.
He put the blame on me,
As he told me it was my fault.
He failed to protect me,
When I needed him the most.
He took his arms away,
And let me fall to the ground.
He shut his eyes,
So he wouldn't see.
He didn't want to see,
It was him this whole time.
He didn't want to see,
The decisions he made.
He didn't want to see,
The choices he made.
He didn't want to see,

How he was to blame.
He didn't want to see,
My emotions I had.
He didn't want to see,
My wounds I had.
I had inside of me,
Because of him.
He didn't want to see,
Even when I tried to open his eyes.
It was easier for him to keep them shut.
I had my eyes shut,
So I wouldn't see him.
I had my eyes shut,
I learned this from him.
I had my eyes shut,
As I looked the other way.
I had my eyes shut,
Until the day they opened.
I opened my eyes,
And I saw him.
I saw this reality,
That I never saw.
I saw that he taught me,
Self-sacrifice.
I learned this from him.
Abandon myself.
Don't have a voice.
Be controlled.
Stay on a leash.
He taught me this,
To have my eyes closed.
I opened my eyes,

---

When I found my own love.
I opened my eyes,
When I found my light.
The light,
He was supposed to help me to find.
Instead, he taught me...
To dim my light.
Dim my light,
And make myself small.
This is what he taught me...
Close my eyes.
I kept them shut,
My whole life.
I didn't want to see this.
This reality.
This illusion.
This façade.
The games.
These games, he took part in.
These games, he taught me.
The day I opened my eyes,
Was the day that I saw...
I saw him with his eyes closed.
His eyes were closed,
My whole life.
How did I miss this?
How did I not see?
How did I miss this reality?
Now that I see,
I cannot unsee.
I am standing here now,
As I see him.

I see him with his eyes shut.
He kept them shut,
As I walked away.
I had to walk away.
I did this for me.

## Burdens And Knives

The root of it all.
This father wound.
The root of it all,
Self-sacrifice.
This root,
I hold.
I hold in my hands.
This root sent pain,
Into my back.
I have carried this root.
Carried in my shoulders,
Into my neck.
This root,
I will put down.
Self-sacrifice I have been holding.
Holding in my hands.
Given to me...
Straight from my dad.
He showed me this.
He taught me this.
He knows it so well.
I knew it so well too,
Until I fell.
I fell down,
And I couldn't get back up.
I didn't have his hand to help me up.
Reaching for his hand to help me up.
Grabbing and reaching,
For his hand.

Please,
Where is it?
Where is your hand?
Please help me up,
I can't get up.
I was kicked down,
Down to the ground.
I couldn't get back up.
I needed him to help.
Reaching and reaching,
For his hand.
It was never there,
My whole life.
It was me that got up,
By myself...
I got myself up,
Each and every time.
I thought he was there...
He was there every day.
His voice on phone calls.
Phone calls to me.
His voice.
His words,
He was there.
But he was missing in action.
He didn't give me his hand.
I needed his hands to help me up.
I needed his hands to keep me safe.
I needed his protection,
More than just words.
I needed more than just phone calls,
His words on the phone.

Giving me breadcrumbs.
Handing them out.
Handing me self-sacrifice.
*"Here take this."*
This was the action.
The action he took.
*"Here learn this...*
*Learn this from me.*
*Abandon yourself.*
*Do not use your voice.*
*Shove it down.*
*Stay small.*
*Stay down there.*
*Stay here with me.*
*This is the way,*
*The way I have showed you,*
*Your whole life.*
*These words.*
*Pretty words."*
Phone calls each day.
I thought this was love.
These were my breadcrumbs.
He handed me self-sacrifice,
From the minute I was born.
He taught me to live in an illusion.
Live in this façade.
He handed me my mask.
*"Here wear this.*
*You will need it your whole life.*
*You will need it in this house.*
*Put your mask on,*
*And just shut your eyes.*

*Keep them shut.*
*Keep them closed.*
*Do this your whole life.*
*Do not interrupt my illusion I live in.*
*If you do,*
*You will be scolded,*
*I will punish you and dismiss you.*
*Do not interrupt how I live...*
*You must sacrifice yourself,*
*To be my daughter.*
*I will not deal with your problems.*
*I will not deal with your voice.*
*The reality you want,*
*I will shut it down.*
*Your words you speak,*
*I will turn the other way.*
*The truth you tell,*
*I will deny it every time.*
*It is my way or no way,*
*It is all your fault.*
*This black and white thinking,*
*Is my way.*
*I will blame you...*
*So, I don't take responsibility.*
*I will never take accountability...*
*The burden is yours.*
*I will hand this to you,*
*For you to carry.*
*These burdens are yours,*
*I want you to hold them.*
*Hold them for me,*
*And shut your eyes.*

---

*Be just like me,*
*Keep your eyes closed.*
*I will allow knives to be thrown.*
*Thrown right at you.*
*I allow them to be thrown,*
*As I look the other way.*
*These knives have left wounds.*
*Wounds in you.*
*Wounds I won't help you with.*
*Wounds I will leave you,*
*To deal with.*
*Deal with your wounds.*
*Deal with these knives.*
*Deal with these burdens.*
*And keep your mask on!"*
I take these burdens.
I take them slowly off my shoulders…
I grab them in my hands,
And I lay them at his feet.
I take the knives out…
Slowly out of my back.
I take these knives,
And hold them in my hands.
I take every single knife,
And I lay them at his feet.
I put my mask down…
I am giving it back.
These burdens,
These knives.
My mask.
I give them all back.
"These are yours.

These were never mine.
Mine to carry.
You can have your burdens.
Please look at these knives.
These knives that have been thrown.
Thrown at me,
My whole life."
I give him my mask back.
I give it all back.
A choice I must make...
I am doing this for me.

# Self-Sacrifice

She lived a life of self-sacrifice.
Putting herself aside.
Every single time.
Put herself aside.
This is how she lived,
For such a long time.
She lived a life of self-sacrifice.
She didn't know any other way.
Leaving herself,
For everyone else.
Making herself small,
So they could feel big.
Going out of her way,
To make sure they were okay.
Meeting their needs,
While sacrificing hers.
Doing for them,
When she had nothing left.
Self-sacrifice is what she knew.
She knew it so well.
Not speaking up,
So they would feel fine.
Holding it all in,
Out of fear.
Fear of punishment.
Fear of blame,
Fear she would be turned on.
Turned on and left.
Abandoned and punished.
This was the game.

She played their game.
She joined in,
For them.
She forgot about herself,
Because her heart was so big.
She had love for everyone else,
And left nothing for herself.
Emptying herself out,
Abandoning herself.
Putting herself aside,
One last time.
Never again...
Will she do this to herself.
Never again,
Will she leave herself.
Never again,
Will she sacrifice herself.
Just to please everyone else.
"Please them.
What do they need?
Are they happy?
Is everyone good?"
What about her though?
What about her needs?
What about her?
She forgot about herself,
While thinking of everyone else.
She didn't hold herself,
While she held everyone else.
She didn't love herself,
Because she was too busy loving everyone else.
She didn't have her own worth,

Because she was worried about theirs.
This ended with hurt.
This ended with pain.
Heartache and heartbreak.
Her falling to the ground.
She didn't understand,
Why it hurt her so much.
She didn't understand,
Because this is all that she knew.
She didn't understand,
Because this is how she was loved.
They loved her like this.
They only loved her,
When she was meeting their needs.
They only loved her,
When she sacrificed herself.
The day she stood up.
The day she spoke up.
The day she held her own worth.
Her own worth in her palm.
Her palm of her hands.
This was the day...
The day she realized,
This love in herself.
She would find the ones,
Who loved her just for who she is.
Not for what she could do.
Not for meeting their needs.
Not for silencing her voice.
Not for sacrificing her being.
Not for playing their game.
She would find the ones,

Who just let her be.
No expectations.
No pressure.
No blaming.
No scolding.
She could finally just breathe...
Just be...
She was finally free.

# Keep Her Around

Have her stay silent.
Push her away.
Shut her voice down.
Make her go away.
Make her feel crazy.
Make her feel small.
Keep her on a leash.
This leash of control.
Keep her around...
Hand her these breadcrumbs.
Use this as bait.
Keep her around...
She's easy for us to use.
Use to meet our needs.
She's easy for us to abuse.
She is so naïve.
She abandons herself.
Just to feel loved.
She does this for us.
She does it for us.
This is why we like her.
This is why we approve.
This is why we keep her around.
This is why we push her around.
Stomp on her when we are in a bad mood.
Pick her up when we need her.
Put her down when we don't.
When she is not meeting our needs,
She is no good.
No good to us.

This is when we leave.
This is when we gaslight her.
Blame her.
Put it all on her.
She will carry our shit.
She always has.
She doesn't hold us accountable.
She never speaks up.
She lets everything slide.
She plays our game.
She plays it so well.
She joins in it with us.
And then we throw her right under the bus…
So she can be crushed.
Crushed and ran over,
While we stay up.
We stay up on our pedestal,
Feeling so good.
We stay up on our pedestal,
With a smile on our face.
As we smear her name,
And come up with a smear campaign.
We do this to feel good.
We love to feel good.
We live in denial.
This delusional world.
We live in this illusion.
Putting on a façade.
Wearing our masks.
Putting on a show.
A show for the world.
The whole world to see,

As we play our roles.
We are stomping on her.
Shoved her to the side.
Blaming her.
Stomping on her.
As long as we feel good…
We live in this façade.
We live like this.
We love it like this.
We refuse to come down.
We love our mask.
We wear our mask.
We wear it every day,
As we play our game.
We love our game.
We have two kids,
Who walked away.
Walked away from the games.
Took off their masks.
They stopped playing along…
And it is all their fault.
We will say this until the end.
We will not give up.
Give up on our world.
Give up on ourselves.
We love it like this,
Living without our kids.
We will trash their name.
Let them look bad.
Throwing knives at them,
While we look big.
Keep throwing the knives,

While they stay away.
Stay far from us.
Far from our games.
We like it like this.
We like to feel big,
While our kids feel small.
Their job is to do for us,
And the day they stop...
Is the day they get stomped on.
Crushed and stomped on.
Used and abused.
Kick them down,
While they are not around.
We will never stop to think...
Was it something we did?
Because we don't want to see...
We like it like this.
We like it our way
...only one way...
And that is it.

# Sacrifice Myself

I am mending this wound.
This unworthiness wound.
This feeling of unimportance.
This feeling of feeling afraid.
Afraid to speak up.
Afraid to be seen.
Afraid to become who I was always supposed to be.
Releasing this now.
Releasing these beliefs.
These beliefs that weigh me down.
Releasing this pain.
I cry these tears.
I have committed to myself.
I am done with self-sacrifice.
Sacrificing my needs for everyone else.
Sacrificing my own love,
To pour it all out.
Leaving myself drained,
While they leave filled up.
Feeling afraid,
To be who I am.
Cowering down,
So they could feel big.
Becoming small,
So they would feel good.
Forgetting who I am,
To be there for everyone else.
Help them.
Love them.
Be there for them...

Sacrifice myself.
This was my role.
Allowing myself to be controlled.
Fitting into the mold.
The mold they laid out.
Reading from the script.
The script they gave.
Accepting my breadcrumbs,
That they use as bait.
Sweeping everything away.
Burying my feelings.
Suppressing it all.
Living a life.
A life for them.
The fixer.
The helper.
The giver.
The girl with no boundaries.
The girl with no voice.
Just do as I am told,
And be controlled.
Putting my worth in everyone else's hands.
I hold my worth now.
I hold it close.
Close to me,
Tightly.
Tightly in my hands.
And I will never let it go.
I deserved unconditional love.
It is what I deserved,
The whole entire time.
I deserved my own love.

I was taught...
Sacrifice myself.
Or love would be taken away.
Transactional love,
Was the reason for my self-sacrifice.
Leave myself behind,
So that I would be loved.
Leave myself behind,
And worry about everyone else.
Leave myself behind...
That is what I was taught.
That is what I was shown,
Sacrifice myself,
Or love will be taken away.
Sacrifice myself...
This is how I lived,
For a very long time.

## At The Bottom

Starting at the beginning.
No one,
Around.
No one,
I know.
No one,
But me.
Starting at the bottom.
Starting at the beginning.
Starting fresh,
With no one but me.
I am in my new world,
All alone.
I am in this new world,
Not knowing where to go.
Which way do I go?
Which way do I turn?
How do I do this?
How do I see?
See which way is for me.
Feeling it out.
Feeling every inch of the way.
Listening for signals…
Not turning back.
Following my gut.
Listening to myself.
I hear my voice.
My voice of intuition.
This will not steer me wrong.
I trust in this.

I feel a surrender.
A surrender in me.
Carrying the weight.
The weight of the world.
Carrying the weight,
Of discomfort and pain.
Carrying the weight,
Of what is not for me.
Carrying this weight...
Carrying it around.
I feel this in my body,
Every single inch.
This weight I carry,
I need to put down.
Trust in my journey.
Trust in myself.
Trust in the doors.
The doors that will open,
When I put this weight down.
This weight, I am carrying.
I am carrying this around.
I don't want to be here.
I need to get out.
I just don't know how.
Which way is my way out?
These tears from my eyes...
Falling from my face.
These tears of knowing.
That I need to get out.
These tears of knowing...
I can't do it anymore.
These tears of knowing.

I am in the wrong world.
These tears of knowing.
I am carrying this weight.
I am carrying this around.
I need to put it down.
When do I set it down?
When will I know?
I will listen intensely.
I will listen for it.
I will call in a sign.
A sign to know.
Know when to leave,
And where should I go?
I know I will feel it.
I trust in this.
But my body can't take...
Much more of this.
This knowing.
This calling.
This being in the wrong place.
I don't belong here...
I need to get out.

## This Inner Peace

Sitting in this inner peace.
This inner freedom.
This inner acceptance.
Sitting here,
I am silent.
Silence.
This quiet.
This stillness.
This radical resilience.
Oh, wow.
This acceptance.
This beauty.
This vibration.
This serenity.
This calm.
This knowing.
This beam.
This beam of light.
This beam of love.
My love.
I am holding in the palm of my hands.
This softness.
This glowing.
This freedom in me.
I am holding my own love.
I am holding it.
I am keeping it,
And spreading it to the world.
Spreading my vibration.
My healing.

My love.
This inner peace I have chosen.
Chosen for myself.
I will keep on choosing...
Again and again.

## This Cage Of Generational Trauma

You failed to protect me.
You did not keep me safe.
I stood by you,
My whole life.
I stood by you,
I gave you my heart.
I stood by you.
I thought that was my job.
I stood by you,
As I put myself aside.
I stood by you,
As I kept you on your pedestal.
Holding you up.
Higher than me,
Giving you praise,
To keep you lifted...
Higher than me.
Giving you praise,
To keep you content.
Holding you up,
Higher than me.
My whole life,
I held you up.
Until the day,
I found my own love.
I found my light.
I had to let go.
Let go of you.
Let go of your pedestal.
Let go of the grip.

I stopped lifting you up.
I stopped giving you praise.
I stopped putting myself aside,
To set myself free.
Free of the burdens.
Free of that cage.
That cage I was in.
I was in my whole life.
That cage you kept me in.
That cage,
I left.
You are still there,
Along with all of your friends.
That life,
I left.
I am free.
I made a choice.
A choice for me.
I made a choice,
To set myself free.
I made a choice,
To leave you behind.
I had to get out.
Get out of that cage.
I made a choice.
A choice for my freedom.
A choice for my love.
A choice for myself.
A choice I will make,
Over and over again.
A choice I made,
To sacrifice.

Sacrifice that cage.
That cage of control.
Everything I knew...
All that I know.
I will sacrifice that,
So that I can be free.
I say goodbye to you.
I say goodbye to me.
The part of me,
That had love for you.
That had love for that cage.
That cage of control.
That cage of self-sacrifice.
That cage of transactional love.
That cage was never mine.
That cage was yours.
You made it yours,
Because you chose to stay.
That cage is not mine.
I will leave it behind.
Goodbye to you now,
As I walk away.
Goodbye to you now.
I am free.

# The Weight Of My Family

I am carrying this weight.
This weight of the world.
I am carrying this weight.
I am putting it down.
This is not mine.
This is the weight,
I have carried my whole life.
This is the weight.
The weight of my family.
The weight of their trauma.
This is what they have carried.
The weight they have carried,
For so many years.
Generations and generations.
This weight on my shoulders.
This is their weight.
The weight of self-sacrifice.
Sacrifice yourself.
This is what I was taught.
This is how I was raised.
I will carry this weight,
Until I put it down.
Passed down to me,
They handed it to me.
I took it and held it...
I carried it for years.
I thought this was my job.
This was my job.
The job they gave me.
They expected this of me.

I had to become...
Who they wanted me to be.
Carrying their shit.
Carrying their burdens.
Carrying it all.
Until I say NO.
I am putting it down.
This generational baggage.
This baggage of hiding.
Hiding myself.
This baggage of abandoning.
Abandoning myself.
Sacrificing myself.
Sacrificing my voice.
Sacrificing my needs.
Sacrificing my soul.
I have carried this baggage.
I carried for years.
I am giving it back.
Back to them.
I am handing it back.
I am putting it down.
I am finally going to choose myself.

## This Risk I Take

This risk I take.
I take it for you.
I take it for me.
I take it for them.
I am taking this risk.
I am following my heart.
Leaving society.
Leaving the norm.
Leaving expectations.
Leaving control.
Leaving the box.
Leaving the cage.
Breaking free.
Free from that leash.
"This is the way.
The way to go down...
This is the way."
This is not the way...
The way for me.
The road I am going down,
Is a bumpier road.
This road I am going down,
Is the road into the unknown.
This road I am going down,
Is not even paved.
This road is new.
This is the way...
The way for me.
I found my own lane...
This lane for me.

---

This lane is lonely.
This lane is misunderstood.
This lane is judged.
This lane is looked down on.
I am standing apart.
Apart from the crowd.
I am standing here,
In stillness.
Away from the noise.
I am standing here,
Seeing.
My eyes are wide open.
I see the illusion.
I am taking it down.
It comes crashing down.
The illusion.
The denial.
The façade.
The show.
It is all coming down.
It is coming to an end.
The end of the façade.
The end of the trauma.
This generational trauma,
That I have carried for them.
I am destroying it.
I am not carrying it.
I am shattering the illusion.
These words I speak,
Are shattering the illusion.
Staying in my lane,
As I leave the façade.

Choosing me,
As I become free.
Free of the cage.
Free of the burdens.
Free of self-sacrifice.
Free of control.
Leaving my mask.
My mask with them...
This mask I wore,
Kept me safe.
Safe in a world,
That was not fit for me.
That world was not mine,
I must leave.
Walking away.
Not turning back.
Leaving a world of comfort,
Going into the unknown.
No support.
Just me in my lane.
Off I go,
It is my turn now.

# Pretend

Pretend it didn't happen.
Pretend nothing is wrong.
Pretend like it is all okay.
Pretend,
And shove it all under the rug.
Pretend,
And talk nothing out.
Pretend,
And keep going.
Pretend,
Bury it deep down.
Pretend,
And move on.
Move onto something else.
Pretend nothing happened.
Keep moving forward.
Put on the smile.
Put on the happy face.
Keep going.
Keep going.
Shove it all under the rug.
Shove it so far,
It will never come out.
Shove it,
And pretend.
Sacrifice yourself.
Do it every time.
Put yourself aside.
This generational trauma.
This generational curse.

Shoving it under the rug...
Simply does not work.
It does not work...
Deal with it as it comes.
Stop shoving it under the rug.
Pretending and faking.
It does not work.
Pretending.
Just stop.
Stop with the games.

## It Is A New Start

Looking at yourself.
Yes,
It is hard.
Making time for yourself.
This is a must.
Taking care of yourself.
This comes first.
Loving yourself.
This is the way.
The way to your heart.
The way to a new start.
This is the way.
Commitment to the pain.
Feeling the pain.
The pain that you hold.
The pain that you shoved away.
Your heart,
Holds this pain.
These layers of pain.
Peel back the layers.
Feeling those emotions.
Letting them be.
No judgement.
No control.
No suppressing them.
Burying them deep down.
Keep moving ahead,
Without feeling to heal.
Feeling the pain,
Is not the easy way.

Feeling the pain,
Is a path by itself.
A path less traveled,
By anyone else.
Facing those demons,
Will have you kicked down.
Kicked down to the ground.
Losing what you know.
Losing yourself,
Along the way.
Letting those parts of you go,
Because it is not who you are.
You must let them all go.
Let those parts of you go.
You don't need them anymore.
They are keeping you trapped.
Weighing you down.
Keeping you in your past.
Let those parts of you go.
Yes,
It is sad.
Feel that pain.
Those parts of you,
You learned to love...
Just to let them go.
You appreciate them now.
Because they got you to where you are.
You don't need them anymore.
You are not her anymore.
You are not those girls you once were.
Let go of them now.
Let go of her hand.

---

Let go of the plan.
That plan in your head.
That pretty painted picture,
Let it all just go.
Be here now.
Listen to your heart,
But let that past go.
Loosen your grip.
Don't hold on too tight.
Take that leap.
Choose your heart.
Begin again.
It is a new start.

# The Name Of The Game

I choose me.
I choose me this time.
I choose peace.
This time,
I chose my quiet place.
I choose respect and love,
Over control and assumptions.
Over manipulation and expectations.
I choose kindness and compassion,
Over abuse and mistreatment.
I choose beauty and solitude,
Over chaos and noise.
I choose myself.
I choose my gut.
I choose my love.
I choose my soul.
I choose my heart.
I choose me.
I choose me this time.
I am in control of my life.
I choose quiet.
I choose peace.
I choose this moment.
I choose me.
I choose calm and serenity,
Over noise and insanity.
I choose to live authentically.
I walk away respectfully.
I walk away from what is not for me.
I walk towards what is meant for me.

I leave my past.
I put it all behind me.
I put down my mask,
As I walk away from the façade.
None of it works for me,
Not anymore.
I am not who I used to be,
I walk away from it all.
I am leaving the cage.
I put down my script.
They kept me on a leash.
A leash that I stayed on.
My leash I give back,
Along with my mask.
I speak words of truth,
That destroy their illusion.
That break that façade.
Which ends all the chaos,
That has been going on.
Walking away.
Away from the games.
It was all that I knew.
These games were my love.
I don't know how to play now.
Even if I tried,
I would just break down and cry.
Because what I knew was a façade.
What I knew wasn't real.
Transactions were love.
Breadcrumbs were rewards,
Given if I was good.
Disguised as love.

They would be taken away,
If I misbehaved.
Punishments and control,
Led the way.
Live in fear,
If I keep playing the game.
Stay below them.
Always below them.
Hold them up.
Up on their pedestal.
Hold them up high.
Higher and higher.
Higher than me.
I must stay where they put me.
They must feel big.
Bigger than me.
*The name of the game...*
*You must act this way.*
*You must be this girl.*
*You must meet our needs.*
*You must do for us.*
*You must behave.*
*Behave for us.*
*Stay on this leash.*
*This leash of control.*
*You must sacrifice yourself,*
*For us every time.*
*You must not leave this cage.*
*This cage is for you.*
*This cage we put you in,*
*As you play our game.*
*Rules and regulations,*

---

*That you must follow.*
*We will give you this script,*
*A script you will live by.*
*Follow our lead,*
*So that we feel big.*
*The name of the game...*
*You must stay where we put you.*
*Sacrifice yourself.*
*Sacrifice your needs.*
*Over give when you have nothing.*
*You must not have boundaries.*
*You must come when we call you.*
*You must do as you are told,*
*Even as an adult.*
*You must live in our world.*
*You must follow our script,*
*And stay on this leash.*
*You must live with this illusion,*
*Keep up with our façade.*
*You must keep playing all of our games.*
*You must obey the rules.*
*Obey our rules.*
*Because we are in control.*
*We put you here,*
*And that is where you stay.*
*Your words you speak,*
*Must be read from our script.*
*Nice and happy.*
*Always be happy.*
*We do not speak the truth,*
*Because we live with our illusion.*
*Please do not disrupt our illusion,*

*Because you will ruin our façade.*
*If you speak honest words,*
*You are holding up a mirror.*
*A mirror for us to look in,*
*To see ourselves.*
*We do not want to see,*
*What is really going on.*
*We will do everything we can,*
*To put it back on you.*
*We will make you our villain.*
*You are the bad one.*
*You always have been.*
*You ruin everything.*
*You are the villain.*
*You are the bad one.*
*It is always you.*
*We will blame you,*
*So that we feel big.*
*We will never look in the mirror,*
*That is your job.*
*This is your job you are doing,*
*As you walk away from us.*
*You have stopped holding us up.*
*Holding us up on our pedestal.*
*You are now trying to hold us accountable.*
*Accountability is not part of our game,*
*It is not part of our society.*
*There will never be an apology.*
*We will never change.*
*We will stay this way forever,*
*As we make you our villain.*
*We see you walking away...*

*Walking away from our games.*
*These games you don't take part in.*
*Our script has changed on our end...*
*We have made you our main character,*
*As we trash your name and reputation.*
*We call you names and make fun of you.*
*We trash what you are doing.*
*We will never look in the mirror,*
*Because you are the villain.*
*This is the story we are telling.*
*This is part of our illusion.*
*This is part of our façade...*
*This façade we put on.*
*We put on for the world.*
*The name of the game...*
*You must stay where we put you.*
*What people don't see in our façade we put on...*
*Is the punishment we give you,*
*When you stop playing our games.*
*You must stay where we put you...*
*Or we take love away.*
*You must stay where we put you...*
*Or we put the blame all on you.*
*You must stay where we put you...*
*Or we hand out punishments.*
*You must stay where we put you...*
*Or we belittle you.*
*You must stay where we put you....*
*Or we take our breadcrumbs away.*
*You must stay where we put you...*
*This is the name of this game.*
I choose me.

I choose me now.
I have left that insanity.
The grief I feel,
Leaving a world I knew...
Is the heaviest I have felt.
I let it flow through my body...
As I feel it all.
I grieve this façade.
I grieve what I knew.
I grieve the love I did not get.
I grieve those people I love.
I grieve those old parts of me.
I grieve that whole world.
I grieve everything I knew.
I let it all go...
It is the hardest thing I have ever done.
I choose me.
I put myself first.
I commit to feeling this grief,
All of it...
Every last bit of it.
I choose me.
I choose this grief.
After this is over,
I set myself free.

## This Sigh Of Relief, Is Gold To Me

For the first time ever,
I sigh this sigh of relief.
This sigh of freedom...
I am free.
For the first time ever,
On the other side of grief.
For the first time ever,
I believe in me.
For the first time ever,
I believe I can do it.
I can do anything I want to.
I can do anything I set my mind to.
I can go where I want to go.
I put the past behind me,
As I leave a façade.
This façade I lived in.
This façade, I knew.
I leave this behind,
Everything I knew.
I speak my truth now,
Without receiving punishments.
I speak my truth now,
I do this for me.
I choose me.
It is my turn now.
For the first time ever,
I put myself first.
For the first time ever,
I don't sacrifice myself.
For the first time ever,

I sigh this sigh of relief.
This sigh of freedom,
As I leave.
I leave the insanity.
I leave it behind.
I leave the chaos.
None of it was for me.
My body couldn't take it.
My heart couldn't endure it.
I couldn't live it.
I had to choose me.
I chose to leave,
A whole world behind.
I chose to leave,
Everything I knew.
Everything I loved,
I had to walk away from.
I chose to walk away,
Because I had to choose me.
I chose me.
I did this for the very first time.
I sigh this sigh of relief.
I am on the other side of grief.
The other side of pain.
I am standing on the other side,
Looking behind.
Looking at all that I left behind...
Some of it good,
More of it, not.
The good that I left,
Was not worth the pain.
The good that I left,

Was just a transaction.
The good that I left,
I had to owe back.
The pain that I felt,
When I over-gave myself.
I had to over-give,
Just to receive love.
I had to wear my mask,
To receive my breadcrumbs.
These breadcrumbs of love,
That I survived on.
This is what I see,
When I look behind me.
This is what I see now,
This insanity.
This insanity was my normal.
This insanity was my love.
This insanity was my life.
My life for so long.
I had to endure so much pain.
So much grief,
I would feel.
I had to give up,
Everything I knew.
Just so I could breathe in,
This sigh of relief.
This sigh of relief,
Was worth it all.
It was worth the pain,
Every last bit.
It was worth the grief,
I carry with me.

It was worth the heartache.
It was worth my heartbreak.
This sigh of relief,
Is gold to me.
This sigh of relief,
Is all I will ever need.
This sigh of relief,
Is meaningful to me.
The meaning behind,
This sigh of relief...
This meaning is:
I can finally breathe.
This meaning is:
I am free.
This sigh of relief,
Is gold to me.

## All I Would Like For Christmas.

All I would like for Christmas,
Is healing and peace.
Healing from within.
I am turning in my pain.
I am turning in my grief.
I am turning it all in,
Like cash that you give.
Cash that you give,
To buy something nice.
This something nice that I would like,
Is internal peace.
Internal peace...
Breathe in.
Breathe out.
This pain that I will release,
Will bring me this internal peace.
Serenity and bliss.
Calm and still.
I turn it all in,
To get myself this.
All I would like for Christmas,
Is internal bliss.
Bliss filled with peace.
Bliss filled with love.
All I would like for Christmas,
Is to hear the beating of my heart.
Beating for me,
Beating for my love.
Still beating for me,
After the betrayal that I felt.

Still beating for me,
As I let go of my past.
Still beating for me,
As I walked away from the chaos.
The chaos and the noise.
The belittling games.
The hurt in my heart.
The tears that I have cried.
All I would like for Christmas,
Is silence and beauty.
Quiet the noise of the world.
Just for a time,
Please give this to me.
I cash it all in,
To get something nice.
Something nice for myself.
I cash it all in,
To free myself.
I bought myself freedom.
This freedom looks good.
Looks good inside of me.
I am free.
I can breathe.
Oh,
This peace.
This serenity.
I feel this bliss.
All I would like for Christmas...
It looks like it cost nothing.
But it cost me,
My everything.
Everything I knew.

Everything I loved.
All that was familiar.
The only thing I knew...
I turned it all in,
To feel this peace.
This internal peace,
As I became free.
Free from that cage.
Free from that turmoil.
Free from that noise.
I turned it all in,
To get myself this.
Peace I never felt.
Love I never knew.
Unconditional love.
Beauty I never saw.
Freedom, I hadn't lived.
All of this looks like nothing to some.
But to me,
It is everything.
I will take this,
As my only gift.
All I need...
This Christmas,
Is this internal peace.

## This Softness

Remove the expectations.
Remove the outcome.
Remove the plan.
Remove the noise.
Be here now.
Be here in this moment,
With no commotion.
Be here in this moment.
Be here in this silence.
Be here in surrender.
Be here in this quiet place.
Be here with your breath.
Be here with no sound.
Be here with serenity.
Be here with this peace.
You have found this.
Be here in this softness.
The softness of this moment.
Be here without the chaos.
Be here in this stillness.
Be here in all of this.
This complete and total softness.
Serenity and bliss.
Solitude and acceptance.
The fleeting feeling of happiness.
You have found self-transcendence.
Trust in your ascendence.
You have found independence.
You are becoming this.
Trust in this.

---

Surrender to this.
Just be here with this.
This silence.
Be here in this softness.

## The Main Ingredient Is Unconditional Love

Building a life,
Just to take it down.
Building a life,
For it to come crashing down.
Building a life,
A life that I loved.
Building a life.
A life for me.
Building a life,
Built on self-sacrifice.
I built this as the foundation,
While putting myself aside.
I built this foundation,
While I sacrificed my feelings.
I put them aside,
Along with my needs.
For everyone else,
So they would feel pleased.
I put myself aside,
So they would feel good.
So they would feel comfortable and loved,
While I suffered inside.
I put myself aside,
So many times.
I put myself aside,
Because that is what I was taught.
Self-sacrifice.
Self-abandonment.
Self-betrayal.
Becoming small,

---

238 shell.chelle

For everyone else.
Hiding myself.
So that I could fit in.
Fit into what though?
Fit into society.
Fit into my family.
Fit into a world.
A world of rejection.
A world of judgement.
A world full of gossip,
And opinions.
A world of ego.
To fit into everything else.
Except for myself.
Leaving myself behind,
For everyone else.
I built this life,
With these as the foundation.
I built this life,
While saying yes to everything.
Saying yes when I wanted to say no.
Going and doing,
While I needed rest.
Pleasing and smiling.
Pushing through.
Be that go getter...
Do.
Do.
Do.
Finish and succeed.
Accomplish and build.
Win and make more.

Add more and keep adding,
Until there is nothing left.
Nothing left,
But a shell.
This shell.
Of myself.
I can be whatever I want to be.
I don't ever have to fit into society.
Society and the beliefs.
The judgment and opinions.
The norm.
What makes sense,
That just is not me.
It never was.
It never will be.
I will stand on my own,
Because that is who I am.
The black sheep.
The rebel.
The one who stands out.
The girl who "causes" trouble.
The one who says what no one wants to hear.
The one who states the truth,
That no one wants to face.
The one who notices it all,
Every single shift.
The one who goes against the grain.
The one who will never make sense.
The one who can withstand that smear campaign.
The one who is okay with being the villain.
The one who is 1 in a million,
Or 1 in a billion.

---

Or maybe even…
1 in a trillion.
I don't make sense.
I won't make sense.
I will never make sense.
I will live now,
At my own expense.
I am intense.
I am on my own,
I stand out from the crowd.
I am the black sheep.
Not fitting into society.
I never will,
And that is okay.
The only place I need to fit into,
Is myself.
The only person that needs to accept me,
Is me.
The only person that needs to love me,
Is me.
I finally fit in.
Fit into *my world*.
A world I needed to tear completely down,
So that I could rebuild.
Rebild with new foundations.
The main ingredient in this new world,
Is unconditional love.
I left a world of transactions.
A world filled with conditions.
I left my old foundation.
I left it behind.
I built a new foundation.

I started at the bottom,
Sitting with my darkness.
I started at the very bottom,
with all my loneliness.
It was worth it,
Every last bit of it.
Because when I was done,
I was sitting with my light.
I was sitting with my love,
And it was love at first sight.
I was no longer sitting at the bottom.
I was now soaring in the sky,
Holding unconditional love.
This unconditional love,
Set me free.
This unconditional love.
First for myself,
Followed by everyone else.

## True To You

When you walk the path,
Of your authentic self.
When you walk this path,
You won't fit in.
You are not the norm,
In a world full of masks.
You are the black sheep.
This is just how it is.
You have left a world.
A world you knew.
You have left beliefs.
Beliefs that were not you.
You have left behind,
Anything that is not true.
True to you.
True to your soul.
You have found a new path.
You have chosen this,
And many will not understand.
This new path that you will walk...
You will leave behind,
All that you know.
You will walk ahead,
Into the unknown.
You will accept yourself.
This new you.
You have gotten to know her,
And you really like her.
You feel free.
You finally feel love.

You feel your heart,
Beating for you.
You see your soul,
In a clarity you have never seen.
You feel the call.
You feel it in your bones.
You feel it in your heart.
You feel it in your soul.
A call that gets louder.
Louder each day.
You wait with patience,
For the final call.
You wait with patience,
To feel the signal.
The signal you have been waiting for,
All along.
You feel the pull.
You listen for it.
You are connected to your soul.
Your soul will lead you.
Lead you in the right direction.
This direction is for you.
Listen closely,
You will hear it.
You are preparing.
Preparing for the call.
For now,
Keep walking...
Down your path.
Your path of authenticity.
You are learning.
Authentic and true.

---

True to your soul.
True to your heart.
True to you.

# These Are All Hers

She lived with these chains,
Her whole life.
She lived in that cage.
She catered to them.
She became what they needed.
She became their healer.
She became who they wanted.
Who they wanted her to be.
She cheered right up.
She put a smile on her face.
She became happy,
So they would feel pleased.
So they were comfortable.
So they were appeased.
She became someone else,
And left herself behind.
She shoved her voice away.
She put her mask on.
She put herself aside,
A million times.
She put herself aside,
For everyone else.
She buried herself away,
So she could be liked.
So she could be loved.
Loved externally.
Loved by everyone,
Other than herself.
External love will never be fulfilling.
Internal love will guide the way.

---

Love internally,
Set her free.
Love and light are now in her hands.
Her hands are full.
Full with her worth.
Holding her worth,
Close to her heart.
Never letting it go,
Because this is hers now.
Her love.
Her light.
Her worth.
She found her intuition,
Inside of her light.
Her knowing.
Her clarity.
Her acceptance.
Her peace.
Her beauty.
Her joy.
Her serenity.
Her empowerment.
Her freedom.
These are hers now.
These are all hers.

## Your Mold

I don't conform.
I won't conform.
I was made,
To go against the grain.
Never a day...
That I fit in.
Fit into society.
Fit in with the group.
On my own,
And that is just how it is.
I am on my own,
Not being understood.
They don't understand me.
They never will.
Don't even try...
Just stand by my side.
Without trying to fix me.
Without trying to mold me.
So that I fit.
Fit in.
Fit in with you.
Fit into society.
Fit into your mold.
Your mold that you made.
You made this mold.
For me to fit into.
But that is not me.
I will never jump in,
To fit in with society.
No that's not me.

I will leave right away.
The very minute I feel you,
Trying to fix me and mold me.
This feels like control to me.
I won't be controlled.
I can't be controlled.
I will never be controlled.
I will run the very minute,
I feel that control.
Trying to grasp.
Grasp for me back,
As I grow out of your mold.
Your mold that you had.
You had it for me.
You made it for me.
I will never stay.
Stay where you put me.
I feel those grips,
Coming to get me.
I feel that control.
I feel your hands,
Trying to hold me back.
You want me to stay.
Stay with you back there.
You want me to stay.
Stay where you put me.
But I don't belong there.
I never did.
I belong to my freedom.
I belong to my peace.
I belong to my love,
That I found in my light.

The only place I will ever stay,
Is my own soul.
This very place,
Where I hold my own love.
This very place,
That you can't get ahold of.
Because I am so far away.
Away from your grip.
Just let me go.
Let me be free.
All I need,
Is to just be me.
All I need,
Is to just be free.

## This Stillness

Do you feel this stillness?
My stillness.
My solitude.
My silence.
My bliss.
My gifts rise,
As they come to the surface.
My intuition speaks.
My soul,
It glows.
My stillness.
My softness.
My light.
My love.
Do you feel this stillness?
This stillness in me.
Let me just be.
Be here now.
Let me feel this.
I could feel this for eternity.
This peace.
This serenity.
This appreciation.
This acceptance.
This knowing.
This being.
This clarity is arising.
Let me be here.
Be here in this stillness.

Let me just be here.
Be here now.

## I Come Back With Love

When the world keeps going,
And I have stopped.
When the world is loud,
And I am not.
When the world keeps moving,
And I stay put.
When the world has beliefs,
And I have created my own.
When the world has chaos,
I stay in my peace.
When the world has traditions,
And I walk away.
When the world wants you to stay silent,
But I have something to say.
When the world has expectations,
And I have none.
When the world wants an outcome,
And I do not.
When the world wants familiar,
And I go to the unknown.
When the world leads with control,
And I have surrendered.
When the world pushes for answers,
And I don't need a solution.
When the world follows a plan,
I go with the flow.
When the world lives a certain way,
And I live my way.
When the world goes in one direction,
I go the other way.

When the world has a road paved,
I go against the grain.
When the world thinks of the future,
I live in the moment.
When the world wants you to wear a mask,
I take mine off.
When the world wants you to be a certain way,
I become myself.
When the world doesn't understand,
I shrug it off.
When the world conforms,
And I am the black sheep.
When the world lives on the surface,
And I like to go deep.
When the world wants you to be someone you're not,
This is when I show my authenticity.
When the world wants to ignore feelings,
I feel my grief.
When the world wants to judge you,
I let the judgment come.
I hear it.
I see it.
I observe it,
And then I let it go.
When the world tries to fix you,
I say thank you and leave.
When the world doesn't accept you,
It is okay.
When the world is cruel,
I don't play the game.
I lead with peace,
And walk the other way.

When the world changes,
I accept it.
Why fight it?
When the world is black or white,
I go to the grey.
One extreme or the other,
Why is it this way?
Why can't everyone live their own way?
When the world is filled with conditions,
I have none.
When the world is filled with hate,
I come back with love.

# I Am Me

They wanted her in her mind,
But she followed her heart.
They said stay here,
But her body said no.
They said behave,
She said what does that mean?
They said stay put,
She said I will go & be brave.
They said stay quiet,
She said why?
They said sit down,
She said no way.
They said this is how it is,
She said but not in my world.
They said conform.
She said I am free.
They said move.
She said be still.
They said be busy.
She said rest.
They said have a plan,
She said for what?
"I live in the moment,
How do you plan for that?"
They said commit,
She said I can't.
They said permanent,
She said that exists?
They said estranged,
She said I am just over here, feeling free.

---

They said do this,
She said no thanks.
They said these are the rules.
She said I don't really follow rules.
They said follow this path.
She said I'll make my own.
They said you must put up with this.
She said oh, no I don't.
They said these are the traditions,
And she just needed change.
They said stop,
But she must go.
They said think.
She said feel.
They said rigid.
She said flow.
They said do.
She said be.
They said wear this mask,
She turned them down.
They said live in this façade,
She decided to leave.
They said this illusion is yours,
She said it never was.
They said family.
She said friends.
They said judge.
She said love.
Lean in.
Get curious.
Find out why.
They said tell.

---

She said ask.
They said stop being a rebel.
She said never.
They said be someone else.
She said I am me.
They said give up.
She said believe.
They said you can't.
She said watch me.
They said be strong.
She said I am sick of being strong.
They said make sense,
She said why?
They said control.
She said surrender.
They said be silent.
She spoke her truth.
They said be dependent.
She found her independence.
They said stay the same,
She changed in every way.
They said stay small.
She said grow.
They said be nice.
She said be honest.
They said be this.
She said *I am me.*

## This Nothingness.

Fall in love with nothing.
Fall in love with silence.
Fall in love with solitude.
Fall in love with quiet.
Fall in love with rest.
This is where the beauty is.
The beauty of you is here.
You are found in nothingness.
You are found in quiet.
You are found in silence.
You are found in your breath.
You are found in stillness.
You are found in the softness.
The softness of serenity.
The softness of this bliss.
You are found here.
Right here,
In this nothingness.
Hold your heart here.
Right here in this stillness.
Hold your heart here.
Here in this nothingness.
Hold your heart,
As you find your light.
As you find your love.
Right here in this peace.
This peace that you found.
This peace.
This freedom.
This faith.

This love.
Right here,
In this nothingness.
Just be.

## Your Gift

To hide your gifts,
Is to hide yourself.
To hide behind barricades and walls,
Is to close your heart.
To hide who you are,
Is to abandon yourself.
Abandon your light.
This light,
You have been carrying.
It has been there all along.
All covered up.
Covered up by darkness.
Covered up by pain.
Covered up with dust.
Dust and dirt.
This light,
You have uncovered.
This light,
You are holding now.
This light is yours.
No one can take it.
No one can dim it.
This light.
Your light.
Your beautiful heart.
You have been pushed to the limits.
You have been pushed to the edge.
You have been pushed to the darkness.
You have been pushed to face it.
Face your demons.

Face your blocks.
Face your struggles.
Face your pain.
Face your barriers,
You are living behind.
Break them down.
Set yourself free.
The fire is over.
You are shining your light.
Your fear has fallen.
Fallen away.
Your light is guiding.
Guiding the way.
You trust in it now,
More than ever before.
You pushed past your fears.
You let go of the past.
You accept what is.
This is now.
You are finally resting.
You are in silence.
Silence and solitude.
To find your frequency.
Your authenticity.
To find your light.
You have found your love.
You have found your worth.
You have sat in loneliness.
You have sat in your darkness.
You have come to realizations.
You have found compassion.
You have found forgiveness.

---

You have found acceptance,
In this ascendance.
You hold your gift.
You give it away.
This is your clarity.
Your integrity.
Your frequency.
Your authenticity.
You speak words of truth.
You walk away.
You remove yourself.
You walk back to your love,
Every single time.
You are your light.
You are your gift.

## This Table

Sitting at your table,
Still talking about me.
Sitting at your table,
Still gossiping about me.
Sitting at your table,
While I sit at mine.
My name,
Still coming out of your mouth.
My name,
Spoken in a negative way.
Why can't you see the love in me?
Why can't you see the pain I carry?
Why can't you see my purity?
Why can't you see?
And have empathy for me?
Why can't you understand,
That I needed to leave?
I needed to leave,
To heal my pain.
I needed to leave,
To heal my heart.
I needed to leave,
To find my light.
My light wasn't accepted at your table.
My light was dimmed while sitting at your table.
My light was stomped on and used,
While sitting with you.
My light was demeaned and dismissed,
So that you felt big.
My light was turned off,

---

While sitting with you.
I needed to leave,
To find peace within.
I needed to leave that table.
I needed to leave and stay away.
I needed to find my own table.
My own table,
Of love.
My own table,
Of light.
I needed to find my very own table.
A table that doesn't gossip about me.
A table that just lets me be me.
A table that isn't out to get me.
A table that isn't filled with envy.
A table that isn't going to reject me.
A table that isn't using me.
Using me to fulfil their own needs.
A table that sees me.
A table that is filled with safety.
A table that is made up of unconditional love.
A table that has no conditions.
A table that is not made up of transactions.
A table that is filled up of moments.
A table that is filled up of memories and love.
A table that is free of guilt trips.
A table that is not worried about image.
A table that is minimal.
A table that is not filled up with material things.
A table that is not filled up with money and show.
A table that does not turn my light off.
I needed to sit at a table with friends.

Real friends.
The friends that don't talk about you behind your back.
The friends that accept you and your pain.
The friends that accept your boundaries and distance.
The friends that understand and hold compassion.
The friends that don't scold you,
For speaking up.
The friends that don't leave you,
If you don't act the way they expect you to act.
I needed to leave to find this table...
After sitting at a table with bullies my whole life.
After sitting at a table with manipulation and motive.
After sitting at a table to meet everyone's needs.
After sitting at a table with expectations.
After sitting at a table where my light goes unnoticed.
After sitting at a table with no accountability.
After sitting at a table where no one takes responsibility.
After sitting at a table of denial and blame.
After sitting at a table of projection and abuse.
After sitting at a table with masks and facades.
After sitting at a table where everyone is in their ego.
After sitting at a table where everyone has their hearts closed.
After sitting at that table,
I can finally appreciate this table.
This table,
Of love.
This table,
Of flaws.
This table,
Of appreciation.
This table,
Of understanding.

---

This table,
Of compassion.
This table,
Of acceptance.
This table,
Of resilience.
This table,
Of growth.
This table,
Of emotions.
This table,
Of openness.
This table,
I will sit at.
I will continue to sit here,
While you sit at yours.
I will not be going back to sit at that table.
That table of bullies.
That table where my name is spoken,
In negativity.
That table of gossip.
I have left that table,
And I have left it for good.
Next time my name is spoken,
Out of your mouth.
Ask yourself,
Why?
Why do you care?
Why are you exerting this kind of energy?
Why is my name still coming out of your mouth?
The only thing I did,
Was go find a new table.

This new table,
Of unconditional love.

# I See

I see clearly now.
Oh, I see clear.
Oh, I know.
I really know.
And once I see,
I cannot unsee.
And once I know,
I cannot unknow.
I see this big picture.
I understand now.
I feel the energy.
The energy beneath the action.
I feel that energy.
I can feel it right away.
That weird vibe.
I was right.
My gut told me,
Every single time.
I thought I could fix it.
I thought I could change it.
I was holding on.
I was holding onto hope.
Please don't be true.
Please change,
For me.
Please grow,
For me.
These true colors,
I see.
These true colors,

I know.
I see what you can't.
I know what you don't know.
I feel the vibe.
I see the denial.
I let it go.
It is all I can do.
Move on.
Keep going.
Do not give up.
I see now.
You must do it for you.
You must see with your own eyes.
You must know with your own gut.
I see now.
I see this.
I know now.
I know this.
I am on my journey.
And you are on yours.
You are in your own thing,
While I am in mine.
This knowing.
This understanding.
This awakening.
This beauty.
This is what I will give away.
Give to the world.
I see it now.

# From My Heart To Yours

I must choose myself,
And love from afar.
I must choose myself,
And send love from a distance.
I must choose myself,
When my light is dimmed.
I must choose myself,
When the past pulls me back.
I must choose myself.
Raise the bar.
Attract respect.
Break the cycle.
Do not lower my standards.
Do not give in.
Do not give up.
Let go again.
And again and again.
Protect my peace.
Raise my frequency.
Be in my authenticity.
Know my genuinity.
Create alchemy.
Show integrity.
Find my clarity.
Shine in my vulnerability.
Lead with my femininity.
Embrace my sensitivity.
Surrender to my spirituality.
Accept my insecurities.
Listen for my heartbeat.

My heart beating is my light.
My light is my love.
My love is my beauty.
My beauty is my gift,
That I give away.
This gift will shine,
From my heart to yours.
This gift I give you,
Please receive it with love.
This unconditional love,
From my heart to yours.

## "Let Go Of Her."

Every time you lose,
You become someone new.
Letting go of what was.
Letting go of who you were.
When you let go of love,
You must let go of who you were.
"Let go of her."
This lesson I have learned.
To love is to lose.
To love is to grieve.
Grieving means you have loved.
You love with your whole heart.
To love is to let go.
To let go is to find.
Find this new beginning.
Find who you are now.
Let new love in.
It will feel different this time.
You are not the same.
The same as who you were.
"Let go of her."
& you will be free.

## This Rise

I feel this rise.
This authenticity.
This confidence.
This sense of authority.
Authority over my life.
It is my time now.
I feel this love,
Flowing in my body.
I feel this alchemy.
I feel this bliss.
I feel this all radiating.
I feel it.
I feel this peace.
I feel this beauty.
I feel this flow.
I feel this power.
This empowerment.
This enlightenment.
Oh wow.
I feel all of this.
I feel this energy.
I am soaring.
I have released my sadness.
I have released my madness.
I have released my chaos.
I have released my wounds.
I have released my pain.
I have released my fear.
I am sitting with trust.
Pure surrender.

My heart is beating.
My soul is waiting.
I am ready to let love in.
I let love in.
One breath at a time.
I let it in.
I feel it rise.

## She Chose Love

She healed her heart.
She healed herself.
She healed for her.
She healed for her dreams.
She gave everything up,
So that she could be free.
She walked away,
From what dimmed her light.
She walked away from self-sacrifice.
She built up her worth,
From being thrown down.
Kicked down and stomped on,
By people she loved.
She needed to leave,
What dimmed her light.
She needed to leave,
So she could find peace.
She needed to leave,
So she could be free.
Her walls came down,
One my one.
Her walls came down,
With each tear she cried.
Her walls came down.
Her heart was pounding.
She felt her heart,
After shutting it down.
After shutting it off.
After giving it away,
To people who didn't deserve it.

---

To people who took it.
To people who hurt it.
She gave it away to everyone else.
She didn't even see it,
Because this is what she was taught.
This is what she knew,
Until the day she held her heart in her very own hands.
She felt it beating.
She cried tears of love.
Love she hadn't felt.
Because she shut her heart down.
Her heart was beating.
It was her that repaired it.
Each crack.
It was broken.
It was so, so broken.
She held it and loved it.
She picked up each piece and held it.
She handled it gently.
She protected it.
She cried.
She cried and cried.
She kept on crying.
This was her release.
Release it all.
She felt her pain,
Each layer that was there.
She let it all go.
She set herself free.
She finally stood there,
Holding her heart.
She finally stood there,

Feeling it beat.
Beating and beating.
She felt this love.
This love for herself.
This,
She had never felt.
She stood there at the end.
She cried tears of joy.
Her fear,
She left.
She left it behind.
She chose love this time.
Love over fear.
She will choose love,
Each and every time.
She let herself be.
Be with herself.
She let herself love.
Love herself.
She let herself shine.
Shine her light.
She set herself free.
Free with her love.

# You Were The One

You were the one,
I looked up to.
You were the one,
Who was supposed to keep me safe.
You were the one,
Who I loved each day.
You were the one,
Who betrayed me in the end.
You were the one,
I trusted with my heart.
You were the one,
Who broke it.
You broke it into pieces.
You ripped it into shreds.
You broke my heart,
When you turned on me.
Because you didn't want to see.
You didn't want to hear the truth.
You were the one,
Who taught me…
"Do not use my voice."
Because when I did,
I was not believed.
I was not heard.
I was not understood.
I was punished and belittled.
I was demeaned.
You were the one,
Who was supposed to teach me,
To stand up for myself.

You were the one,
Who was supposed to be there for me.
You were the one,
Who should have guided me.
You were the one,
Who taught me self-sacrifice.
Sacrifice myself for everyone else.
Sacrifice myself so they would feel pleased.
Sacrifice myself,
No matter what.
This is how you love me.
You love me,
Only if...
Only if I stay in the cage you put me in.
You love me...
Only if I behave.
Stay on my leash.
Read from my script.
Follow the script...
Each and every word.
This is when you love me.
I choose me.
I choose me this time.
I taught myself this,
When you broke my heart.
You tore my heart into pieces,
And couldn't look at yourself.
You expected me to just get up and pretend.
Pretend nothing is wrong.
You expected me to fawn.
Just as I did,
My whole life.

---

I spent my whole life in a trauma response,
Because I had so much fear.
I released that fear.
Every last bit.
I chose love this time.
I chose myself this time.

## Stranger In The End

You were my best friend,
That turned into a stranger in the end.
Stabbed me in my back,
Handing me more betrayal to feel.
All because I was me.
I finally showed myself.
I spoke up for myself.
I said enough is enough.
I stopped playing games.
I spoke words of truth,
That you didn't want to hear.
I stopped abandoning myself,
Something that you should have taught me.
You betrayed me in the end,
After being my best friend.
The one I looked up to,
Who I had up on this pedestal.
I have taken you down now.
I can look in you in your eye...
Put my head down,
And keep walking.
Walking right on by,
Like I don't even know you.
Like you are a distant stranger.
I loved you with my whole heart.
I want you to know.
I would have done anything for you,
Because that is who I am.
You were my best friend,
Who betrayed me in the end.

The one I looked up to.
The one who should have stood by my side.
A distant stranger to me now.
The one I walk by.
I did not hold my head high...
Because it killed me inside.
It broke my heart all over again.
My heart shattered a million times.
In that second that you walked by.
My heart into pieces again.
I had to pick them back up.
This,
I have done a million times.
I looked down,
As you walked by.
I looked down at the ground,
Because I was broken inside.
For that one second that I saw you.
I sat,
As I watched you.
As I let my heart break...
It broke into a million pieces.
You have this power over me...
Because you were my best friend.
My father,
My whole life.
My father,
Who betrayed me in the end.
This is why I walked right by,
Saying to myself...
"You are not safe."
You are not safe in my eyes.

This realization had me broken,
In that second that I looked down.
I looked down at the ground,
As you passed me by.
Like I was nothing to you.
Like I was not a daughter to you.
That moment,
Looking down at the ground.
Was the moment I made myself safe.
The very first time,
That I chose myself over you.
I have said my goodbyes,
To self-sacrifice.
This time,
I chose me.
Even though it broke me inside.
I had to choose me,
Because you did not keep me safe.
You were my best friend.
This quality in you,
I just could not see.
This denial, I was in.
This illusion, I see.
I would have done anything for you...
But it was not reciprocal for you.
You did not keep me safe,
So I gave this to myself.
I chose myself over you.
I chose me,
Not you.
The very first time,
Although it killed me inside.

I pick up each piece.
Each piece of my heart.
That broke,
As I looked you in your eye.
That broke,
As I walked by.
Each piece I pick up...
I chose me this time.

## This Light Of Peace

Through the pain.
Through the weight.
Through the heaviness.
Through the depths.
Through the shadow.
Through the dark.
I found surrender.
I found forgiveness.
I held acceptance.
I sent out love.
I held it all in my heart.
I dropped the weight.
I put it all down.
I emptied it out.
I released my pain.
I cried my tears.
My heart,
It cracked.
I felt it tear.
The sorrow flowed.
Flowed throughout.
Throughout my veins.
Throughout my soul.
The sorrow left,
As soon as I saw.
I saw it.
I held it.
I really loved it.
Give it love,
And send it out.

---

Bring in acceptance.
Find forgiveness.
Bring in more love.
Let it in,
As I let it go.
I let the light in,
As the darkness left.
I held my light.
This light,
So bright.
This light of love.
This light of peace.

# Where My Peace Resides

My peace is my clarity.
My very own clarity.
My peace is my movement.
My movement into love.
My peace is my vibration.
My vibration of my heart.
My heart beating in the stillness.
This stillness that I have found.
My peace is my acceptance.
My bliss.
My forgiveness.
My peace is my understanding.
My compassion.
My foundation.
My peace is my aura.
My aura is my safety.
My quiet.
My serenity.
My integrity.
I open to my spirituality.
I create alchemy.
I trust in my intuition.
I surrender to it all.
Surrender has carried me through.
Through the darkness,
As I collected what I needed.
What I needed was forgiveness.
What I needed was acceptance.
What I needed was connection.

---

Part ways from separation.
I am connected.
Connected to the sky.
Connected to the trees.
Connected to the rain.
Connected to nature.
Connected to God.
Connected to love.
Connected to you.
Connected to me.
Connected to it all.
Connected to the high vibrations.
These high vibrations kept me afloat.
These high vibrations,
I love.
I held each vibration.
I held them close to my heart.
I filled myself up.
I will never let them go.
I took each one and loved them.
I replaced piece by piece.
I replaced my pain and hurt.
I replaced my heartbreak.
I let it all go,
As I found what I needed.
What I needed was healing.
What I needed was love.
What I needed was peace.
I found my peace.
I found my clarity,
As I left the noise.

As I became still.
Inside of stillness,
Is where my peace resides.

# This Wholeness

This wholeness.
This wholeness in me.
This wholeness in my heart.
I feel so complete.
This wholeness.
This serenity.
This wholeness.
I feel so connected.
This wholeness is what I am holding.
I am holding it in my hands.
Tightly in my hands.
My heart.
Each piece that had broken.
Each piece I picked up.
Each piece I held.
I held it and loved it.
Each piece,
I replaced.
Each piece,
I picked up.
Each piece,
I cherished.
Each piece,
I held.
I gave each piece unconditional love.
Each piece was not forgotten.
Each piece was remembered.
Each piece was acknowledged.
Each piece was treated with kindness.
Each piece I put back,

After feeling the sadness.
After feeling the grief.
After feeling the madness.
After feeling the chaos.
After feeling the heartbreak.
After feeling the betrayal.
Ater feeling the pain.
Each piece I put back.
After each piece was seen.
After each piece was heard.
Seen and heard…
Loved,
By me.
Each piece I picked up.
Each piece I put back.
Each crack in my heart,
Is remembrance of strength.
Is remembrance of my resilience.
I never gave up.
I hold my heart up.
I hold up this wholeness.
I hold this forgiveness.
I hold this acceptance.
I hold this vibrance.
I hold this beauty.
I hold me.
My heart is me.
My whole heart,
I hold in my hands.
I hold it up.
I let it shine.
Shining with love.

Love for me.
Love for all.
We are all connected.
We are all one.
Hold your heart up,
With me.
Our hearts,
We hold.
Hold them up.
Let them shine.

## My Spirit Guides.

She told me strength.
Strength and power.
This is the answer.
My calling has been answered.
Answered by her.
My intuition.
She spoke to me today.
Her answer is here.
I have prayed for an answer.
An answer to my prayer.
She answered me today.
I heard her loud and clear.
She told me strength.
She told me power.
She told me this is needed.
Needed as I soar.
I will soar with my wings.
I have faith in my heart.
I listen to her closely.
I listen for her voice.
Sitting with silence.
No noise.
No chaos.
Peace and serenity.
Bliss and divinity.
Surrounded in my own energy.
I call in my spirit guides.

## Your Body Holds The Wisdom

Your body tells all.
Listen.
Silence.
Let your body guide you.
Let your body give.
Give you everything.
Everything you need.
Let your body love you.
Let your body hold you.
Let your body lead.
Let your body move.
Let your body release.
Let your body give you peace.
Let your body breathe.
Let your body bring in spirituality.
Let your body be.
Let your body speak.
Speak to you in ways.
Ways you have never heard.
You have never heard this language.
This language your body speaks.
This wisdom your body is giving you.
Listen so tenderly.
Listen to each sensation.
Listen to each whisper.
Listen to each piece of wisdom.
Your wisdom is all inside.
Quiet the noise.
The noise of the world.
Quiet the distractions.

Quiet the sounds.
Listen to the silence.
Listen to this bliss.
This bliss your body is giving you.
Let it all in.
Your body will tell you.
Everything you need to know.
Your body will tell you.
All you have to do is listen.
Listen for it.
Listen for the signal.
This signal you have been waiting for.
It is coming very close.

## Let It All Go

Let it all go.
Let her go.
The girl you were.
The girl who got you through.
The girl who stood strong,
As she lost it all.
The girl who stood strong,
As she watched her life fall.
Her whole life fell apart.
She had to repair her whole heart.
Her whole life shattered,
She could barely stand up.
Trying to hold on.
Trying to explain.
Trying to save him.
Trying to ask for help,
As she tolerated abuse.
Shoving everything down.
Shoving it to the side.
Trying and trying,
As she was shut down.
Shut down over and over.
Shut down so many times.
Ignored.
Dismissed.
Gas lit.
Her voice was not heard.
Running in circles,
After people she loved.
Running in circles,

To try to fix it all.
Running in circles,
Until she stopped.
Running in circles,
Until she gave it all to herself.
Looking for it externally.
Leaning on people she shouldn't have trusted.
Leaning on people who kept her small.
Kept her beneath them,
So they could feel big.
Kept her beneath them,
So they can walk their walk.
She stopped giving to them,
And started giving to herself.
You are honoring her now...
But you must let her go.
Let go of the fighter.
She fought until she couldn't.
She cared until she didn't.
She loved with her whole heart.
She gave out all of her love.
She was the giver.
She was the lifter.
She was the go getter.
She was the fixer.
The lover.
The doer.
The leader.
Miss independent.
Meeting everyone's needs,
Leaving nothing left for her.
Let go of her hand.

---

Her time here is through.
You feel it in your bones.
You feel it in your breath.
You feel it in your heart.
It is time to let her go.
It is time.
Time for her to go.
It is time.
Time for you to be.
Be someone new.
Whoever you decide to be.
Let go of it all.
Let it all go.
Let it all fall.
Let it all be.
Let her go.
Set yourself free.
You are now open for vulnerability.
You open your heart.
You are open for connection.
You are open to love.
You feel like a new girl.
A new girl who attracts respect.
A new girl who embraces new opportunities.
A new girl showing her authenticity.
A new girl with boundaries.
A new girl who creates alchemy.
A new girl who operates spiritually.
A new girl who is fierce and brave.
Honest and trusting.
Loving and open.
A new girl who has outgrown this space.

This space that she is in.
This space that she has built.
This space that she has loved.
This space that gave her healing.
This space that gave her peace.
This space that gave her self-esteem.
This space that gave her love.
Love for herself,
As she healed.
Picked up each piece of her heart.
Picked up each piece.
Each piece of pain.
Picked up each piece to hold it and love it.
Hold it and nurture it.
Love it and replace it.
Replace the pain.
Replace it with love.
Love and acceptance.
Peace and forgiveness.
Freedom and abundance.
Gratitude and confidence.
Empowerment and bliss.
Faith and happiness.
This is who she is now.
Grieving all that she was.
Grieving all that she had.
Grieving all that she loved.
Grieving and grieving.
So much grieving.
Putting it all down now,
To follow her heart.

## These Wings

These wings I have earned.
These wings are mine.
These wings make it,
So that I can fly.
Fly above.
Fly away.
Fly free.
I will not stay.
Letting go.
Once again.
Let it go.
Fly away.
Set it down.
I am not meant to stay.
My freedom came.
Came with a cost.
Letting go of all that I knew.
Letting go of all that I loved.
My freedom came,
After feeling the pain.
The pain that I sat in.
The pain that I felt.
The pain that I knew.
I knew it well.
Betrayal and loss.
...then I fell...
Fell into my darkest days.
Fell into my darkest path.
Fell into my darkest parts.
My shadow,

I met.
My shadow,
I loved.
I had to find love for it all.
I had to do this during my downfall.
To fall is to rise.
Rise again.
Pick myself up.
Each and every time.
Pick up the pieces,
Once again.
Make a new choice.
Choose again.
I choose me.
I come first.
I choose me this time.

## I Must Walk Away

I choose me.
I choose me this time.
I rip my mask off.
I throw it to the ground.
I decide now.
I decide for me.
I decide to walk away,
From disrespect and blame.
I decide to walk away,
From control and abuse.
I decide to walk away,
From what brings me down.
I decide to walk away,
From what dims my light.
I decide to walk away,
To save myself.
I decide to walk away,
I am doing this for me.
I decide to walk away,
To preserve my love.
I decide to walk away,
To protect my heart.
My heart is open now.
I must walk away,
From those who break it.
I must walk away,
From those who betray it.
I must walk away,
From those who stomp on it.
I must walk away,

From those who use it.
I must walk away…
Away from the games.
Away from the blame.
Away from the abuse.
Away from the masks.
The masks and the facades.
I must walk away.
I must choose me.
I choose me this time.

# This Aura Is Hers

The darkness has turned to light.
Her soul has released the weight.
Her soul has let go.
Let go of the old,
Her soul was on fire.
Her soul was hidden.
Hidden by layers.
Layers of pain.
Her soul has appeared.
She leads with her soul.
Her voice.
Her leader.
Her intuition is here.
She feels.
She receives.
She leads.
She loves.
She shines her light.
She flows.
She goes.
She surrenders.
She stays.
She is still.
Inside of stillness is where she found her soul.
Quiet.
Silence.
Her breath.
Her heart.
Her light.
Her love.

The quiet.
The calm.
The solitude.
This bliss.
She radiates this aura.
This aura is hers.

## Your Power

When you are out there walking...
Walking with no support.
You have left what supports you.
You have left your circle.
You have left what you know.
You have left this support.
When you have left what you know...
Everything you know...
There is a strength that shows up.
A strength that no one knows.
A strength that no one understands.
A strength that holds you up.
A strength that shows up.
A strength that stays.
A strength that will never go away.
A strength that won't leave you.
Leave you while you are in pain.
A strength that comforts you.
Comforts you and holds you.
Nurtures you and loves you.
A strength that sees you.
Sees you at your weakest.
Sees you at your lowest.
A strength that builds you.
Builds you up higher.
Higher than you have known.
Builds you up better.
Better than you have known.
A strength that wraps you.
Wraps you up with light.

A strength that guides you.
Guides you through the mess.
A strength that loves you.
Loves you no matter what.
A strength that only you know.
You will stand in this truth.
This is your power.
A power that shines.
A power that gives.
Gives you your light.
This power.
Your strength.
That will always shine bright.
This strength is your support.
Your support that you bring.
You bring it.
You carry it.
You do not let go of it.
You show up with it,
Wherever you go.
This is all you need.
This is your power.
This power inside.
Inside of you that comes.
Comes whenever you call.
Comes whenever you need.
Comes when you feel weak.
Comes when you feel down.
Comes when you collapse.
Comes when you have nothing to give.
Comes when you have lost your will.
This power.

Your strength...
This is your support.
Your support is your foundation.
Your roots,
That hold you up.
Your light,
That stays bright.
Shining a cast,
Onto the world.
The world can feel it.
The world can see it.
The world knows it.
This is what you carry.

## Sometimes...

Sometimes the people you love the most...
You have to let them go.
They hurt you more than they love you.
They don't fit in with your soul.
Sometimes you have to leave,
When it breaks your heart.
Sometimes you have to go,
To set yourself free.
Sometimes you have to shut the door,
So that you can protect your peace.
Sometimes you have to turn your back,
So that you can let go and release.
Release what dims your light.
Release what breaks your heart.
Release abuse and mistreatment.
Release what is not for you.
Sometimes you were born into,
A place where you don't belong.
Sometimes you have to leave,
All that you know.
Sometimes you outgrow,
Everything you know.
Sometimes you aren't following the right path,
And you have to get off.
You must create a new one.
Sometimes this new path,
It feels so wrong.
Sometimes you don't know which way to go.
Sometimes you have to sit and wait.
Sometimes you have to sit in the pain.

Listen to every word.
Listen to every sensation.
Listen to every cry.
Listen to your heart.
Sometimes what your heart says,
Doesn't make any sense.
Listen to it all,
So that you can finally surrender.
Sometimes you must take a risk,
And each risk you take...
Will guide the way.
Each risk you take.
Each step you make.
Each breath you take.
Brings you closer and closer,
To where you must end up.
Creating this new path.
Heading right into the unknown.
You have no idea why.
It doesn't make any sense.
Embracing who you are.
You are the black sheep.
They don't understand.
You don't make any sense.
You have become unpredictable.
You have become unreachable.
You are unbreakable.
Sometimes you have to let go,
Because it is holding you back.
Sometimes you have to close the door,
Because you can't heal staying where you are.
Sometimes the people you love the most,

Are the ones who use you.
Sometimes the people you love the most,
Are the ones who betray you.
Sometimes the people you love the most,
Are the ones who can't see you.
They just see themselves,
And that is just how it is.
Sometimes you have to have acceptance.
Sometimes you have to offer forgiveness.
Sometimes you have to have compassion,
While they are trying to bring you down.
Sometimes you have to stay silent.
Sometimes you use your voice.
Sometimes the ones you love the most,
Are not the ones standing by your side.
Sometimes the people you love the most,
Are the ones who disrespect you.
Sometimes the people you love the most,
Are the ones who don't love themselves.
Sometimes their pain blinds them.
Blinds them from reality.
Sometimes their pain takes them over,
And there is nothing you can do.
They don't want to see what you see.
And what you see,
You cannot unsee.
This leaves no choice…
But to leave.
Sometimes your greatest strength,
Is learning to walk away.
Sometimes your greatest power,
Is learning not to stay.

Sometimes your greatest victory,
Is choosing yourself.
Sometimes choosing yourself,
Is really saving yourself.
Saving your heart.
Saving your worth.
Saving your light.
Saving your soul.
Sometimes your greatest pains,
Help set you free.
Sometimes your deepest heart breaks,
Are brought to make you see.
Sometimes you must be the villain,
So that you can sit with peace.
Sometimes it all happens...
Just the way it's supposed to.
Sometimes it all happens...
So that you can learn to surrender.
Surrender and just be.
Sit in solitude and be free.
Believe in yourself.
Shine your light.
Hold onto your love,
And never let it go.

## I Remember Your Face

I remember your face.
Your eyes meet mine.
I remember your hands.
Your hands holding mine.
I remember your spirit.
Your spirt with mine.
I remember your heart.
Your heart beating with mine.
I remember who you were.
The you that I know is gone.
I remember you though.
Who you used to be.
I remember it all.
I remember your laugh.
How did it get to be this way?

# Intention

To set an intention.
To set an invitation.
An invitation to my aura.
An invitation to my field.
An invitation with no expectation.
No outcome.
An intention with no expectation.
Intention.
There is no outcome.
Intention.
Just a will.
A will within you.
Intention.
A vibration.
A fluency.
A feeling.
A knowing.
A direction.
A decision.
Intention of being.
Being here now.
Being in beauty.
Being in staying.
Being in watching.
Being in stillness.
Being in quiet.
Being in silence.
Being in movement.
Being in breathing.
Breathe in.

Breathe out.
Being.
Relaxing.
Serenity.
Peace.
Intention is the direction.
The direction of a moment.
Staying in each moment.
This moment,
Right now.
Intention is the meaning.
The meaning of doing.
To do with intention,
Is to be mindful of the action.
This action with meaning.
Meaning and understanding.
This power.
This force.
This force of intention.
To set.
Set this intention.
A force.
An energy.
This authentic vibration.
Genuine.
Reality.
Breathe in.
Breathe out.
The knowing of why.
Why you are doing this?
Why do you want this?
Why do you feel this?

---

Intention is beautiful.
A beautiful energy.
Intention is connection.
Connection from your heart.
Follow your intention.

## This Femininity

The darkness has turned to light.
Her soul has released the weight.
Her soul has let go.
Let go of the old.
Her soul was on fire.
Her soul was hidden.
Hidden by layers.
Layers of pain.
Her soul has appeared.
She leads with her soul.
Her voice.
Her leader.
Her intuition is here.
She feels.
She receives.
She leads.
Oh, this femininity.
She loves.
She shines her light.
She flows.
She goes.
She surrenders.
She stays.
She is still.
Inside of stillness is where she found her soul.
Quiet.
Silence.
Her breath.
Her heart.
Her light.

---

Her love.
The quiet.
The calm.
The solitude.
This bliss.
She radiates this aura.
This aura is hers.

# Go

To stay in the familiar.
To stay in the comfort.
To stay with what you know,
You will never grow.
To stay where it is unhealthy,
Because that is what you know.
To stay where you shrink,
Because that is what you're used to.
To stay where you validate.
Validate those around you.
To stay where you lift.
Lift those who need it.
To stay where you empty.
Empty yourself out.
Emptying your energy.
When you know you must go.
Go to somewhere else.
Go to somewhere new.
Go to where you receive.
Receive what you need.
You have outgrown this space.
This space that you know.
You have outgrown this place.
This place where you have stayed.
You have outgrown it all,
And it really breaks your heart.
You must grieve all of this,
To go where you belong.
You must grieve this life you built.
You must let go of it all.

Let it all go,
Detach and you will know.
Once you grieve and let it go,
The feeling will come to your soul.
This deep inner knowing.
That you have been waiting for.
This deep inner calling,
That you have been hearing each day.
Louder and louder it gets.
It started as a whisper,
It started as just one word.
Go.
This word from your intuition.
Go.
Every minute of every day.
Go.
"But where do I go?"
...you will feel it inside of your body.
...you will feel it inside of your soul.
Go.
...you will just know.
Each day that passes,
Louder and louder it becomes.
Waiting and waiting.
Resting and feeling.
Waiting and waiting.
Here inside of stillness.
Go.
Louder so that you can hear,
You no longer can ignore this.
Don't worry...
Your dreams will appear.

You are open to receive now,
After all the letting go.
You have made space now,
It is no longer unclear.
Your feelings of grief will dissipate,
And slowly disappear.
You will feel where you belong.
Your heavenly atmosphere.
You will feel it with your heart.
You will feel it inside of your soul...
This is when you will know.
This word go,
Will finally make sense.
This word go...
It will soon be time.
This word go...
This is your calling.
This word go...
This is your ending.
This word go...
Is also your new beginning.
This word go...
You will feel in your soul.
You will know when you know.

## It Hurts To Walk Away

Choosing yourself is not easy.
It is not painless.
It hurts to walk away,
From people you love.
It hurts to walk away,
From people in pain.
It hurts to walk away,
From people who can't see.
Can't see their own pain.
Can't see their actions.
They can't see that they hurt you.
They can't look at themselves.
All they can do,
Is paint you as the villain.
They just cannot see,
And that hurts to walk away.
It hurts to let them be.
Let them be where they are.
It hurts to put yourself first,
When you love with your whole heart.
It hurts when you see their face.
Their face inside your mind.
You see their face in your dreams.
It hurts to leave them behind.
It hurts when they don't know why.
They don't understand.
They just cannot see.
They just have no idea.
They weigh on your heart,
With everything you do.

They weigh on your soul,
As you walk away.
This is a weight that you carry,
With you every day.
This is a weight that no one can see.
Because all they see is your light.
All they see is your strength.
They have no idea what it cost you,
For your light to shine.
For you to have this strength.
It cost you your all.
Everything you loved.
Everything you knew.
It cost you your heart.
Mend and repair.
This is what you have done.
This came with a cost.
Leaving what you loved.
Their faces engrained in your mind,
As you leave them behind.
They don't know why.
They can't understand.
They don't have the tools.
Choosing yourself has you choosing pain.
Which pain do you choose?
Pain if you stay.
Pain if you go.
Either way it is pain.
If you stay...
You betray your soul.
If you go...
You are choosing grief.

---

Betraying yourself?
Or do you grieve what you know?
Grieving as you walk away,
As you choose your soul.
As you choose your heart.
As you choose your light.
This light that shines onto the world,
Which hides all your pain.
The pain they can't see.
This pain you will face,
As you walk away.
You carry this with you...
Every single day.
You carry this weight,
As you walk away.

# First Step

Give it up.
Let it go
It is time to say goodbye.
This life doesn't fit,
With who you are now.
You feel it in your heart.
You feel it in your bones.
You feel it in each inch of you.
But you don't know where to go.
Where do you go from here?
You are in this unknown.
You know you are at an ending.
You are at this crossroads.
But which way do you go?
What is it supposed to look like?
What is it supposed to feel like?
You are ready to take action.
But you don't know what is next.
You are waiting here in surrender.
This softness.
This bliss.
You are waiting for an answer.
An answer that isn't here
You will just sit here now.
Waiting in this peace.
You have found your femininity.
Inside of this uncertainty.
You rely on your spirituality.
You trust in your intuition.
You are ready to take this step.

This step you have been waiting for.
After all the grief you have felt.
This step is waiting for you.
This next step.
Put one foot in front of the other.
And take this step…
One step at a time.
Just one step.
This is where it begins….
Taking this first step.

## These Wings You Wear.

You have been here all along.
Waiting to be seen.
Waiting to be heard.
Waiting to feel deserved.
Waiting to feel important.
Waiting for your worth...
Your worth to finally be honored.
Your worth to finally be held up.
Your worth to finally be seen.
Seen the way it should.
You have been here waiting.
You have been waiting all this time.
Putting up with bullshit.
Being used and bullied.
Being abused and controlled.
Being picked over.
Being stomped on.
Your heart has been beaten down,
Multiple times.
Your heart has been torn up,
So many times.
Your heart.
Your worth.
Your light.
Your love.
It is finally your turn,
To believe in yourself.
It is finally your turn,
To be seen for who you really are.
It is finally your turn,

To show your worth.
It is finally your turn,
To choose yourself.
Choosing yourself,
Over everything else.
Choosing yourself,
No matter what.
Trusting yourself,
Like never before.
Letting your intuition soar.
You have earned your wings.
These wings you wear.
You have earned these wings,
That will carry you through.
Carry you through,
This unknown you are in.
Listening to it all,
Tuning into your intuition.
Putting the weight down.
Putting it all down.
Whoever comes,
Comes.
Whoever goes,
Goes.
Whoever stays,
Stays.
Whoever dislikes you,
Let them.
Whoever bullies you,
Walk away.
Whoever tries to control you,
You will not stay.

Whoever tries to dim your light,
You will shine even brighter.
Your light shines brighter,
Each time you walk away.
Each step you take,
As you hold up your worth.
As you hold up your love,
And you don't let it go.
The only thing you hold onto now,
As you walk into the unknown.
You are in full surrender,
As you have let everything go.
Your eyes are open wider,
Than they've ever been before.
Your eyes finally see clear,
As you have left the noise.
Silence, serenity, and solitude,
Are with you as your tools.
You will listen to your intuition,
And follow your soul.

## You Are Here For You

Stand proudly in your truth.
Stand proudly in your love.
Stand proudly with your worth.
Stand proudly,
Shining your light.
Let this be a strength,
That guides you through the storm.
Keep rising,
When you just want to fall.
Keep rising,
No matter what.
Keep going.
Don't stop.
As hard as it is.
You have found your resilience.
You have found your vibrance.
You have found your power.
Do not let your light be dimmed.
Stand in your power.
Rise above again.
You are not here to become small.
You are not here,
For everyone else.
You are here for you.
So stand in that truth.
You are here.
You are here for you.

# The Warrior Of Your Life

When you get tired of fighting.
When you are out of explaining.
When you are the glue,
That keeps it all together.
When you are worn down.
When you are burnt out.
When you are tired of putting in all the effort.
Trying and trying.
It was all one sided.
It was you.
It was you.
You were the only one fighting.
You wanted it to work.
You wanted it to be good.
You wanted to help.
You wanted to love,
But it wasn't received...
You were kicked down and deceived.
You were betrayed.
You were beaten down.
You were bullied and knocked down,
Over and over.
Trying and trying.
Fighting and fighting.
Trying to save,
Trying to fight.
Trying to fix.
You burnt yourself out trying.
And now you've got nothing left.
You are walking away.

This time for good.
No turning back.
The trust is gone.
You stood back up.
Little by little.
You have lifted yourself.
Little by little.
Your light has come back.
Little by little.
Breathe in.
Breathe out.
Never again,
Will you put your worth in anyone's hands.
Never again,
Will your light be burnt out.
Surrounding yourself,
With people who see you.
Surrounding yourself,
With people who love you.
Surrounding yourself,
With your very own love.
You fought like hell,
To be standing where you are.
You fought like hell,
To be holding your heart.
You fought like hell,
For this new start.
Cheers to you...
For all the times,
You fell apart.
You always got back up,
No matter what.

You stand here now,
You have earned this place.
You are the warrior.
The warrior of your life.

## She Is Not The Same

They see.
They see what they want to see.
Only what they want to see.
Instead of seeing what is reality.
The denial is real.
Those rose-colored glasses.
The illusion they live in.
That lens they look through.
They see what they want to.
What they want is good.
Good only good.
They see only one side.
They won't see them.
Only her.
She is the bad one.
She always has been.
They don't see her light.
They don't see her love.
They don't see her feelings.
Their lens is fogged.
They don't see her,
For who she really is.
They just see her,
For what she can do.
They just see her,
To meet their needs.
They just see her,
As something to use.
They have their own walls.
They have their own eyes.

They have their own picture.
That they paint of her.
They put her in a box,
And this is where she stays.
They put her here,
And this is right where she remains.
Until the day.
The day she changed.
She lives for herself.
She protects herself.
Doing and doing,
For everyone else.
This can't go on...
Not anymore.
She will live her life.
She will meet her own needs.
She will feel her feelings.
She will invest in herself.
She will learn the word no.
She will learn to rest.
She will learn to do,
What is best.
What is best for her.
She will listen to her intuition.
She will follow her heart.
She will not stay,
If she has to go.
She will not partake.
Partake in the games.
She needs to feel understood.
She needs to feel safe.
She needs to be herself.

---

She will not shrink.
Not anymore.
She will not become,
Who they want her to be.
She will not do it all,
Just so they feel pleased.
She will release her guilt.
She will release her shame.
She will put down her anger.
She is just not the same.
She has changed.
Just like that.
Poof.
She's gone.
Just like that.
Poof.
She's back.
She has returned.
As a different girl.
She has returned.
She is not the same.

## Sometimes The Answers Are Not Here

Sometimes the answers are not here.
Sometimes you are in the midst of the storm.
Sometimes you are standing in the chaos.
Sometimes you are there...
There in the unknown.
The unknown needs surrender.
Surrender needs trust.
Trust needs love.
Love needs you.
You will bury yourself in the music.
The sounds of the universe.
The signs all around you.
You relax in this peace.
The answers are not here yet.
Just you sit and wait.
You will feel it,
When your time is here.
You will feel it.
The answers are not here.
Surrender and just be.
This is your purpose.
Surrender into bliss.
Be in this softness.
Just be still.
In this stillness.
Just hear this silence.
Do you see this serenity?
This serenity isn't here yet.
You feel it in your heart.

This inner knowing that you carry.
This inner knowing inside of you.
Just listen and it will tell you.

## She Stopped.

She stopped being walked on.
She stopped being used.
She stopped being controlled.
She stopped being abused.
She started using her voice,
Even when it shook.
She started walking away,
When her light was dimmed.
She accepted her grief.
She felt it all.
Put her heart back,
Piece by piece.
She started speaking up.
Speaking her truth.
She started being honest.
Honest with herself.
She started closing the door,
On a life that wasn't hers.
She started having faith.
Having faith in herself.
She started detaching.
Detaching from it all.
Detaching from everything.
Except for herself.
She started feeling peace.
Peace within her heart.
She started feeling drawn.
Drawn to a new life.
She was so connected.
Connected to her heart.

She was so connected.
Connected to her intuition.
It was after her pain and tears,
That she found her healing.
She found her love.
She found her light.
She found her gifts.
She found her voice.
She found her choice.
She took all of this...
Packed it all up.
She jumped in her car,
With all that she learned.
She drove away,
Not looking back.
Headed right into where she belongs.
Where she belongs...
In her new life.

## Standing Up For Herself

Standing up for herself,
Triggers their shame.
Speaking her truth,
Triggers their guilt.
Sharing her story.
Using her voice.
Holding them accountable,
And walking away.
This causes friction.
This causes a rift.
Making waves.
Rocking the boat.
Being brave.
Being the rebel.
Being authentic.
Speaking up,
Causes trouble.
Causes emotions.
Emotions in them.
These are their problems.
They are not hers.
She gives them back,
One by one,
She won't take them on,
Not anymore.
She hands them their problems.
Directly,
"Here you go."
She has dropped her fear.
She has let go.

She will not be brought down.
She will not stay small.
She will not be bullied.
She will not be controlled.
She has put her foot down.
She takes her power back.
She keeps her light on.
It shines so bright.
She walks right into...
The love of her life.
The love of her life,
Is her own heart.
The love of her life,
Has cost her,
Her all.
She holds it up high,
Along with her worth.
She holds both of these,
And won't let them go.

## This Beautiful Mess

This beautiful mess.
This chaos.
The struggle.
The fall.
The flaws.
The darkness.
Our breath.
Such a beautiful mess.
It is in the mess that we open our heart.
It is inside of the mess that we find our beauty.
It is inside of the mess that our light turns on.
To sit in the dark.
To feel the pain.
Let it rise.
Let it be.
Let all just be.
Let go of resistance.
Let your ego relax.
Let it all rise.
It will rise to leave.
Silence.
Solitude.
Surrender and rest.
Embrace it all,
Inside of acceptance.
I am in love...
With this beautiful mess.

# Simplicity

Lately.
Beauty.
Simplicity.
Divinity.
Tranquility.
Just be.
In this new earth energy.
Feel.
Radiate.
Peace.
Love.
Be you.
Be free.
Let go of who they want you to be.
Be you,
With those that see.
It will become a clarity.
Be you,
Authentically.
Be you,
Wholeheartedly.
Be you,
Unapologetically.
Be you,
Inside of your frequency.
Be in tune with your own energy.
Shine in your femininity.
Show your vulnerability,
As you step into your authenticity.
Leave behind,

Old beliefs and qualities.
Take risks and embrace uncertainty.
Stop trying to fit into society.
Walk away from the insanity.
Build your own community.
Be open for new opportunities.
Send love to all of humanity.
Silence.
Stillness.
Serenity.
This is how you feel free.
This.Is.Reality.
Be you,
Inside of this simplicity.

# I Can Be Me

I deserve to be seen.
I deserve to be heard.
I deserve to be me.
I am worthy.
I have done nothing wrong.
I am not breaking the rules.
I am done walking on eggshells.
I can just be me.
If I want to give.
If I want to love.
If I want to be open.
If I become vulnerable.
Express myself.
I deserve this.
I will become magnetic.
I will attract.
I deserve to be authentic.
I deserve to be free.
I will not sacrifice myself...
Never again.
I can just be me,
Inside of this peace.
This peace,
Is a gift I gave to myself.
This gift,
I will hold.
I will hold it with love.
My peace.
My love.
I can finally be me.

## Your Light Is On

You found your gifts.
You found them in you.
Waiting there inside...
This whole time.
You found your treasure.
Your gold.
Your love.
Your light.
Waiting under the layers.
The layers of pain.
The layers of darkness.
You found your voice,
That was silenced your whole life.
Your truth you speak.
You see the unseen.
You have found your gifts,
Inside of surrender.
Inside of silence.
Inside of the music.
You found your gifts,
Inside of the unknown.
You woke up one day,
And here it all was.
Walking the wrong path,
Until the day you got off.
Until the day you stopped.
You started making your own path.
A new path.
A different path.
Different, than the world.

Different, than society.
Spreading this love.
Spreading this light.
Shining your worth.
Releasing the old.
You are new.
You are not the same.
You are you,
And your light is on.

# I See Myself

I see myself.
I am the black sheep.
I see me,
For who I really am.
I see me,
Without my mask.
I see me.
I am worthy.
I deserve to feel seen.
I deserve to feel heard.
I deserve to release this.
I will heal this wound.
I need to rest.
I need to just be.
I need my own energy.
I need myself.
I need my love.
I need to be nurtured.
Pampered and adored.
I deserve to be helped.
I deserve to be cared about.
I deserve respect.
I finally believe this.
I have dug my way,
Out of a hole.
A hole I was in,
My whole life.
A hole I was in,
With the wrong crowd.
They dug my hole deeper.

Deeper and deeper.
They would rise above me,
On their pedestal.
As I kept getting buried underneath the soil.
Buried and buried.
Smaller, I would become.
Hiding in this hole,
Until the day I got out.
I dug myself out.
I found the right crowd.
The ones who cheered the loudest.
The ones who would fight.
Fight for me.
I deserve this.
The ones who helped me out of my hole.
The ones who kept me from getting back in.
The ones who didn't forget about me.
The ones who stood by me,
As I got out of that hole.
I need rest.
Lots of rest.
I am too tired to put effort in.
I am exhausted.
I need to rest.
I have never given myself this.
I will give myself this,
As I heal this wound.
I will give myself this,
As I love myself.
I will give myself this,
As I sit in my pain.
This pain I was in.

In for so long.
I ignored this pain.
I ignored this sorrow.
I had no idea.
I kept shoving it down.
Shoving it down,
While handing my love out to everyone else.
I kept myself hidden.
My true self.
I kept her small,
And held everyone else up.
I deserve a turn.
This time is for me,
I hold myself up.
I am allowed.

# Inside Of This Simplicity

Rest.
Reset.
Recharge.
Relax.
Just be.
This is your femininity.
Savor this peace.
Your heart is beating.
Your aura is glowing.
You are spreading your love.
Savor this moment.
This moment right now.
No plans.
No noise.
Silence and serenity.
This solitude,
Is so serene.
This solitude.
This peace.
This bliss.
Changing from within,
And no one can see.
Tuned into your own energy.
Tapped into this inner peace.
Let it all come.
Let it all flow.
Let it all change.
Let it all go.
This moment is beautiful.
The clouds in the sky.

The grass that you stand on.
The earth beneath you.
The frequency around you.
Your vibration.
The outer world...
Shrug it off.
Let it all be.
Just as it is.
This.is.acceptance.
Be the light.
Detach.
Disconnect.
Just be,
In your femininity.
Just be,
Inside of this simplicity.

# This Sweet Simplicity

This sweet simplicity.
This unknown is beautiful.
This moment is radiant.
This surrender is so peaceful.
This silence is so quiet.
Breathe in.
Breathe out.
Another moment has arrived.
It passes right by.
Each moment comes.
Each moment goes.
My soul.
My spirit.
My heart.
My love.
Holding it all.
This bliss.
This vibrance.
This energy within me.
My beauty.
My light.
My worth.
I hold this all,
So close to me.
Each moment that comes.
Each moment that goes.
I radiate this peace,
For all of the world.
I stay in my frequency.
I savor my energy.

Each moment that comes.
Each moment that goes.
My peace.
My treasure.
My gold.
My body.
I love all of this...
This sweet simplicity.

## Your Bouquet Of Self-Love

The world is not black or white.
Find your light.
In the grey.
Hold up your bouquet.
Your bouquet of self-love.
So many options.
Which way do you go?
Which path do you take?
The choice is yours.
Yours to make.
Take one step.
One step at a time.
It is a process...
Walk the line.
Up and down.
Around and around.
It won't look perfect.
You will probably fall.
Fall.
Stumble.
Even crumble.
You are creating the path.
One step at a time.
Give yourself a break.
Walk the line.
With your bouquet.
Your bouquet of self-love.
You hold it up.
Take one step.
Another step now.

Keep going...
Don't give up.
Surrender into this moment...
One step at a time.
Holding your bouquet.
Your bouquet of self-love.

# Bliss

Not everyone will like you.
Not everyone will approve.
You have given up your support system.
You have turned it all in,
To sit in your peace.
Turning to surrender,
Leaving control.
Leaving a black and white world,
With nothing but your heart.
Your heart that you have mended.
Your heart that you hold.
You have left this world...
You leave it behind.
You do not look back.
You set everything down.
Everything but your heart.
Surrender and just be.
Trust and you will see.
Believe in yourself.
You do not look back.
You are on the right track.
Falling to your knees.
Setting it all down,
You lay it all down...
At your feet.
Praying and believing.
Letting everything go.
Nothing else matters.
You are here to hold.
Hold yourself.

You have taught yourself this.
You sit in this state of bliss.
Peace and happiness.
Beauty and fulfillment.
Love and worthiness.
Just stay here...
In this bliss.

# Receive

I am open to receive.
Receive vulnerability.
I will receive love.
I have made myself feel safe.
I have taken myself away,
From where my soul does not belong.
I have opened my heart.
I have repaired it.
I have nurtured it.
Perfection,
I have removed.
I am not perfect.
I will make mistakes.
I will say things that are weird.
I will do things that they won't like.
I will need to be alone.
I will need to say no.
I will need to feel my feelings.
I will be honest.
I will speak my truth.
I will be myself.
I want my soul to show.
I want my soul to shine.
I need this in my life.

## You Are You

Stop looking for approval.
Approve of yourself.
Stop looking for it externally.
You are not everyone else.
You are you.
You don't need their approval.
*Do they love me still?*
*After saying no.*
*Did they leave me behind?*
*I set a boundary.*
*I upset them.*
*I wasn't there when they called.*
*I couldn't meet their needs.*
*I had to take care of myself.*
*Are they mad at me?*
*I used my voice.*
*They left me behind.*
You are done with approval.
Approval of them.
If they don't like you,
It's okay.
If they don't like what you say...
Oh well.
If they aren't into you.
Shrug it off.
Become who you really are,
And you will find your tribe.
Say what you want to say.
Set it all down.
Lay it all out.

---

Disagreements happen.
Mistakes will be made...
And it's all okay.
Looking for love,
From everyone else.
Looking for love.
Looking for acceptance.
Acceptance from them,
*Will they accept me?*
*This new me.*
*Will they accept me?*
*Just as I am.*
*Without the perfection.*
*Without my mask.*
*Will they accept me,*
*And my vulnerabilities?*
*Will they accept me,*
*With my sensitivities?*
*Will they accept me,*
*With my empathy?*
*Will they accept me,*
*Authentically?*
*Will they accept me,*
*And my reality?*
*Will they accept me,*
*If I say too much?*
*Will they accept me,*
*When I speak my truth?*
*Will they accept me,*
*Or will they reject me?*
It's okay if they reject you.
It's okay if they don't accept you.

It's okay if they decide not to love you.
It's okay because you love you.
It's all okay...
Because you are you.

## ...And That Is Really It

I can't do small talk.
I don't care about what is on the surface.
I want to go deep,
Because that is me.
I want vulnerability.
I want reality.
Take the masks off.
I love depth.
I want to talk about your soul.
Your dreams.
Your struggles.
Your emotions.
I want to talk deep...
Because that is me.
I can't talk about the weather.
I can't talk about the car.
I don't care about your title.
I don't care about materialism,
Or the money that you have.
That big house that you live in...
And all the stuff you own.
I want to know what's real.
Real inside of you.
I want substance.
I want strength.
I like talent.
Your art.
Your values.
Your virtues.
Your emotions.

I love softness.
Show me your heart.
Show me who you are,
At your core.
I can't do fake.
Take off your mask.
Bring me your vulnerabilities.
Bring me all your fears.
Tell me how you have healed,
And what you have done to grow.
I can't sit and talk about what isn't real.
Tell me what your triggers are.
Tell me who you are.
Who you really are,
Not what you pretend to be.
I don't want to be in an illusion.
Live in a delusion.
Get out of that fake space you are in,
And drop into reality.
Bow down to your ego.
Leave your mask behind.
Stop trying to protect yourself.
Those walls need to come down,
Show yourself finally.
Let yourself be seen.
I am not here to talk about the shoes that you bought.
I am here for the magic.
The magic.
The light within,
What lights you up?
I am here for reality...
Deep conversations.

Fulfilling connections.
The pain.
The love.
The beauty.
All of it...
And that is really it.

# What A Beautiful World.

Rest my body.
Rest my mind.
Rest my spirit.
Rest my soul.
My body speaks.
My heart beats.
My spirit sways.
My soul is at peace.
Bring me to nature.
Bring me to the sun.
Bring me to the water.
Bring me to the moon.
Bring me the earth.
The dirt in between my toes.
Let it rain.
Rain on me.
Let the wind blow.
Let the sun soak.
Soak into my skin.
Let the moon glow.
Glow above me.
Let the leaves fall.
Fall over me.
Let the flowers bloom.
Bloom around me.
Let the water rise.
Let the waves break.
Let the earth shake.
Let the mountains be.
Let nature exist.

All around me.
Breathe in.
Breathe out.
This air in my lungs.
The fires I have survived.
The water that has brought me healing.
The earth that I walk on.
Breathe in.
Breathe out.
What a beautiful world.

## Find Those People

Find the people who lift you.
Who inspire you.
Who cheer you on.
Who love you.
Find the people who motivate you.
Who push you.
Who challenge you to be better.
Find the people who accept you.
Who validate you.
Who make you feel safe.
Find the people who take action.
Who see.
See clearly.
Who hear you.
Who understand you.
Who don't use you to meet their needs.
Find the people who make time.
Make time for you.
Find the people who let you just be.
Find the people who let you change.
Change into whoever you want to be...
Whenever you feel like changing.
Find the people who forgive.
Find the people who speak.
Speak up when something is wrong.
Find the people who don't shove it all under the rug.
Find the people who are direct.
Find the people who love.
Find the people who let go.
Let go of grudges that they have.

Find the people who are willing.
Willing to hear your truth.
Find the people who accept you.
Accept you for you.
Find the people who have faith,
And believe in you.
Find the people who apologize.
Find the people who take accountability.
Take responsibility.
Who have integrity.
Who have beautiful qualities.
You love all of their vulnerabilities.
Find the people in the community.
Who have love for all of humanity.
Find the people who light you up.
Find the people who don't make it all about them.
Find the people who let you say no.
Who don't punish you,
And blame you.
Who don't attack you,
And dismiss you.
Who will ignore you,
And betray you.
Find the people who don't hurt you.
Find the people who hug you.
Take you in and trust you.
Find the people who love you...
Sincerely.
Genuinely.
Unconditionally.
Find those people.

## A Clear No

When everything turns into a no.
A hard no.
A direct no.
A clear no.
This is the sign.
The sign it's time to go.
Nothing in alignment.
Not anywhere.
Not here.
Not there
This is a for sure a sign to go.
Clarity is here.
You are trusting the unseen.
You are the queen.
You hold your gifts inside of you.
You will bring them with you.
You keep saying no.
Keep moving forward.
Keep going...
Proceed on.
Proceed on with your life.
No one understands.
They can't feel you.
They can't see you,
For who you are now.
You have gone so deep.
So deep inside you.
You have this depth,
That no one else knows.
You have this glow,

That everyone sees.
They are drawn to it.
They want it.
They keep on grabbing for it.
Shut them down.
Say no...
And off you go.
Disconnect.
Detach.
Onto the next.
What is for you,
Is within you.
Your heart.
Your soul.
Connect to that place,
And never, ever let go.
Detach and let go,
From the external world.
Disconnect and leave.
Everything is left behind.
These people.
These connections.
You have outgrown them.
It is lonely here.
It is time to move on,
Everything is pointing to your new life.
When are you going to listen?
You are hearing no.
No. No. No.
Over and over.
You keep saying no.
No to this.

No to that.
This isn't it.
Either is this.
Friends and people.
Take in this loneliness.
You are fulfilled when you are alone.
You find meaning in yourself.
Keep going inward.
You will find the answer.
For now say no...
Again and again.
You will know...
When it is time to go.

# I Am The Queen

I am the queen.
I stand on my throne.
I am lifted up.
Higher and higher.
I am lifted.
Higher and higher.
I am the queen.
I am wearing my crown.
I say no to this.
I say no to that.
No this is not me.
No...
Not anymore.
No,
I am done.
I am done putting up with this.
I am done putting up with that.
I am done with the putdowns.
I am done with the games.
I am done with condescending behavior.
I am done being chased.
I am just done.
I am wearing my crown.
My crown I put on...
As I walked away.
Walked away from disrespect.
Walked away from the turmoil.
The chaos.
The drama.
I will walk away.

I am not playing around.
I have been kicked down to the ground.
I have been walked on,
And stomped on.
And now I am done.
I am the queen,
And I am wearing my crown.
I respect myself...
I am not playing around.

## Step Up To Your Throne

Not belonging.
Not fitting in.
You are not accepted.
You are not seen.
You are a being.
A being in this world.
This world that doesn't see you,
For who you really are.
This world that lives disconnected.
Disconnected from their heart.
Living in this world,
Of instant gratification.
Living in this world,
Where there is no justification.
Justification for who you really are.
People just want surface.
What's easy.
What makes sense.
What fits in a box.
They don't want to know.
Know your soul.
They don't want to know.
Know who you are.
*Who are you really?*
*Do you even see me?*
Underneath the façade.
Underneath the mask.
Underneath the layers.
Those barricades and layers.
That are standing in the way.

They operate from their ego.
They cannot connect.
They operate without knowing.
Knowing their feelings.
Rushing over rest.
Doing rather than connect.
Focused on the outside.
The outside world.
Focused on the gossip.
Focused on the drama.
Focused on the surface.
Focused on their mind.
Analytical and logic.
What makes sense.
Mind driven,
Not...
Heart driven.
Onto the next...
The next best thing.
They don't want to feel.
They don't want intimacy.
They don't want depth.
No deep connections.
Just many interactions.
Interacting and filling up.
Filling up the space,
With noise and distractions.
Go.
Go.
Go.
Do not sit down.
Unfamiliar with stillness.

---

Unfamiliar with silence.
Unfamiliar with quiet.
Unfamiliar with feelings.
Shut them down.
Not checking in...
Checking in with themselves.
Not listening to their intuition.
Forcing a connection.
Just because...
Because they can't find love.
Love from within.
They can't find solitude within themselves.
They can't find vulnerability.
Vulnerability with themselves.
They can't sit down.
Sit down and feel peace.
They can't feel peace,
Because they are shut off.
Disassociated and numb.
Shut off to move on.
Keep on moving from this thing to that.
How they cope...
How they feel.
Shut if off.
Discomfort is here.
Shut it down
Don't feel.
Just feel fine.
Smile all the time.
Throw themselves into work.
Meticulous and perfect.
Do not get too close.

Keep them at a distance.
Do not share your stories.
Do not share your truth.
Do not be the real you.
Because they may not accept you.
Rejected and hurt.
*My god...*
*That's the worst.*
Just let it come up.
Feel the discomfort.
No. No. No.
Disassociate and run.
Distract and have fun.
Go. Go. Go.
This is the way to cope.
Shove it all away.
Shove it all under the rug.
Just pretend.
Pretend it's fine.
Don't let them see.
See the real you.
*What if they don't like me?*
*What if they reject me?*
*What if they leave me?*
*Don't open up.*
*Keep it all in.*
*What if I'm judged?*
*What if I am not liked?*
*What if it fails?*
Then,
Oh well.
It's okay.

---

It hurts just for a minute.
For a moment.
It will hurt.
And then you get back up.
Get back up and try again.
Get back up...
You are a queen again.
Get back up and adjust your crown.
Step up to the podium.
Step up to your throne.
Because you are the queen.

# I Had To Leave You

I had to leave you.
Leave you there.
I had to choose myself,
Over everything else.
You felt safe.
Safe in that world.
That world of manipulation.
That's where you felt safe.
That world of denial.
Denial and delusions.
One big illusion,
With absolutely no emotions.
I had to leave you.
Leave you there.
You felt safe there.
I will release this grip.
You are in my heart.
This heaviness I feel.
It is you.
It is your love.
I am letting it go.
It hurts like hell.
I can't even breathe.
Crying for days.
I can't even breathe.
Letting you go.
I feel like it's death.
A death.
A loss.
A piece of my heart.

---

A piece of me,
I am leaving with you.
Leaving it with you,
To hold so close to you.
A part of me is gone,
That I will never get back.
This piece of me...
I leave with you.
A piece of me that I had to see.
I had to see her,
Because you never did.
I had to let her go,
Along with you...
I leave you both behind,
With tears in my eyes.
You know what they say...
Love really is blind.
I was blinded by love.
My love for you.
I was blinded,
Just as you were.
I couldn't see,
And neither could you.
I had to leave you.
Leave you there.
You just couldn't see.
See what I saw.
You couldn't see the reality.
You couldn't feel,
What I am choosing to feel.
I am doing this for you.
I am doing this for us all.

Feeling this pain,
That you wouldn't face.
Feeling these emotions,
That you shoved away.
Feeling this grief,
That took you away.
Away from my heart.
You were ripped away from me.
All because...
You just couldn't see.
I loved you so much,
With my whole heart.
I pray for you each day.
I send you my love.
Tears fall from my eyes,
With this distance from you.
You don't understand...
Why did I leave.
You just couldn't see.
See what I saw.
You just couldn't face.
Face what I am.
You just couldn't leave.
Leave that world.
Leave the world you built,
Because it is all that you knew.
It is too late now for you to ever see.
This breaks my heart,
As I leave.
I have left you for good.
I gave you my all.
I helped you one last time,

As I fell...
Fell as I over gave.
You taught me this.
Over giving to save.
Save the ones I love.
Sacrificing myself.
I have learned this lesson.
I have learned it from you.
I learned this from you.
Passed down to me...
We used to be the same,
Until you threw those knives at me.
You threw them at me,
One last time.
One final time,
And it made me see.
One final time.
This was the last time.
I couldn't do it.
Not anymore.
I lost my strength.
I found my worth.
I knew I didn't deserve this.
Deserve this from you.
You were my dad.
You are a stranger to me now.
I feel like you passed.
I grieve for you.
The love that we shared.
The illusion we lived in.
The fake world of manipulation.
Caretaking and denial.

Not facing reality.
Shoving it all down.
Putting on the show.
Wearing our masks.
I have left you now.
Left you my mask.
That is the girl who was your daughter,
Who shoved her pain down.
Just as you did.
Just as you showed me.
You taught me this,
As I hid away.
Each time I showed myself,
You kicked me back down.
I know now...
That this is not what fathers do.
Fathers are supposed to lift you.
Protect you.
Keep you safe.
Hear you and see you,
Each time you speak.
Value and hold you.
Keep you up on a pedestal,
As you shine your light.
It was the other way around,
For you and I.
I had to leave...
I had to choose me.
It is finally my time.
My time to shine.

## Serenity and Love

When you have seen so much chaos,
All you want to be with is peace.
When you know the darkness,
You appreciate the light.
When you have been betrayed,
More times than you can count.
All you need now...
Is simplicity and love.
All you need now...
Is solitude and bliss.
All you need now...
Is serenity and silence.
You appreciate the quiet,
When you know the chaos.
You appreciate the unknown,
When what you knew failed you.
The familiar.
The comfort.
Your soul didn't belong there.
You have dug yourself out.
So many times.
Trying to run away...
Your whole life.
Trying to get out,
And leave what you knew.
Trying to create peace,
Inside of the chaos.
Trying to find your place,
In a world where you did not belong.
Tearing off your mask,

That you wore for so long.
Seeing everything just as it is.
Seeing it all...
Looking at reality,
Without rose-colored glasses.
Without denial and the illusion,
You are seeing it so clear.
The grief,
Rises from within.
Grieving your life and what you thought it was.
Grieving who you were.
Grieving what should have been.
Grief.
Sadness.
Sorrow.
You know these all so well.
Let it all rise.
Let it all come.
Let it all be.
Let it all leave.
You have left the illusion.
You have left the distortion.
You have left a world you knew,
That you thought you belonged in.
Your soul didn't belong there.
Your soul couldn't survive there.
Your soul couldn't thrive there.
You couldn't shine your light there.
Each time you did,
You were torn down.
Each time you did,
Your light was dimmed.

Each time you showed up there,
You were kicked down.
Kicked down...
You are to stay down.
Stay down and be down.
Do not grow.
Do not shine.
Do not speak.
Do not flow.
This world of belittlement.
This world of pretend.
This world of facades.
This world of masks.
You play your role here.
Stay in your role here.
Put on the show...
And do not grow.
This will be your life,
If you choose to stay.
Illness and disease,
Will become what you know.
Addiction and denial.
Emotional suppression will hold you from growth.
Leave this mask on...
If you must.
Stay the same,
And wear your mask.
Play pretend.
Proceed on with the show.
Putting on the façade.
"Everything is great...
It's great all the time."

Reality is an illusion.
An illusion you create.
A delusion you live in.
Don't let the mask fall off,
And feel your feelings.
Feeling your feelings,
Makes it all real.
Feeling your feelings,
Will lead you to your true self.
Peeling back each layer.
Each layer of darkness.
Each layer of sadness.
Each layer of madness.
Each layer of chaos.
Peeling back the layers...
Will lead you to your soul.
Peeling back each layer,
Will bring you to peace.
Peeling back each layer,
With bring you to serenity.
Serenity and love,
This is what you choose...
When you leave the world of chaos.

# Her History

Her history of opening her mouth.
Her history of seeing the unseen.
Her history of breaking the rules.
Speaking the truth.
Being the rebel.
Being the truth teller.
Being the one,
Who calls all the shit out.
Being the black sheep.
Being the one who stands out.
Going against the grain.
Not following the path.
Not playing the game.
Asking all the questions...
To communicate.
This is the biggest problem.
The biggest problem of all.
Trying to understand.
Instead of attack.
Trying to lean in,
To work it all out.
Not pushing everything down.
Not shoving it aside,
Shoving it all under the rug.
Addressing the problem.
The problem at hand.
Addressing what is happening.
Addressing what is real.
Addressing the illusion.
No.

"I will speak up now."
Her history of knowing.
Knowing the truth.
Her history of leaving.
Leaving the game.
Her history of seeing.
Seeing the problem,
Not living in the illusion.
Pointing out the delusion.
The disfunction.
The chaos.
The abuse.
The mistreatment.
Standing up for herself,
When they want her to fall down.
Stay down.
Be down.
She better stay small.
She is not allowed to have feelings.
We love to make her pout.
She cannot open her mouth.
And if she does,
We will punish her.
Demean her.
Stomp on her.
Belittle her.
Abandon her.
Her history has gotten out of hand.
This has got to stop.
She finally put her foot down.
Once and for all.
The games will not be played.

Her love is for herself now,
Rather than giving it all out to the world.
Freely given because that is who she is.
Her history of loving.
Her history of fighting.
Her history of fixing.
Her history of caretaking.
Her history of being.
Being the one...
The lover.
The fixer.
The pleaser.
The doer.
The caretaker.
Those days are over.
Her history of being stomped on and used.
Her history of being abused.
Her history of trying to make them see.
Trying to fix it.
Trying to be noticed.
Trying to be loved.
Those days are over.
Her grief for herself is pretty extreme.
Leaving people behind.
The ones who don't love her,
Just as she is.
The ones who don't accept her.
The ones who silence her.
The ones who belittle her.
The ones who manipulate her,
And pretend that they didn't.
The ones who want her to fit into their mold.

Their illusion.
Their game.
The game they want to play.
The game they want her to perform in.
Her performance is done.
Her role she has put down.
Her history of all of this,
Is now in the past.
She blows all of them a kiss,
As tears flow from her eyes.
She blows them a kiss,
One last time.

## Each Fleeting Moment

Each fleeting moment.
This moment now.
It is over.
A new one.
A new moment arrives.
A new moment now.
Right now.
Here again.
Another moment,
Passed.
A new one.
A new beginning.
It is over.
Let them come.
Let them go.
Over and over.
A new one now.
I don't know you,
Not anymore.
Each moment I change.
Each moment I am new.
Each moment comes.
Here I am again.
This new girl.
Freedom in each moment.
Letting go of the last.
Welcoming a new one.
Letting go of this one.
Accepting the next one.
Presence.

I am present.
Right here.
Right now.
Silence.
Serenity.
Tranquility.
Heavenly.
Solitude.
Quiet.
This moment that arises.
It passes,
Once again.
Another moment here.
It is gone,
Once again.
Over and over.
Again and again.
Letting go again.
Letting this in to let it all go.
Beauty,
Divinity.
Lovely.
Purely.
Oh.
This clarity.
Give this all to me.

## Surrender Into Love

The sunlight.
The moonlight.
The sand on the beach.
The sounds of the waves,
Crashing at my feet.
I feel so alive,
With the sun on my face.
I feel so soft,
Like I just want to float.
Fall back and land.
I am ready to fall.
Fall into love.
I am ready to love.
I am ready to trust.
Trust love again.
Trust in myself.
Trust once more.
Again and again.
I am ready to surrender.
Surrender into love.

# She Will Hold Your Hand

Appreciate her,
Just as she is.
As she is today.
As she is tomorrow.
She becomes a different person,
In each moment.
She will be a different person,
Whenever she chooses.
Love her as she is.
Love her as she comes.
Stop trying to fix her.
Stop trying to change her.
She is beautiful,
Just as she is.
Appreciate her flaws.
Appreciate her differences.
Appreciate everything.
Her all.
Her heart.
The way she is,
Is magnetic.
The way she is,
Is unique.
This is what makes her special,
Just as she is.
Accept her as she comes...
She is different than most.
Love her as she is...
She is the queen of her throne.
She has her own process,

Different than most.
She knows what works.
Works for her soul.
They haven't gone through.
Gone through her darkness.
They haven't moved through.
Moved through what she had to move through.
Who are they to fix her?
Critique her?
Change her?
They haven't walked her path.
The rough path she has walked.
They haven't had to cry,
The tears she has cried.
They haven't had to lose.
Lose what she has lost.
They have never seen.
Seen what she saw.
They have never repaired.
Repaired what she had to.
She is different from them.
Just as they are different from her.
She has not known,
What they had to know.
Just as they don't know,
Everything she knows.
She has collected lessons.
Different than them.
She shares them with the world,
With a smile on her face.
She still manages to smile,
While carrying the pain.

They don't know what she carries,
Because she does not show it.
She carries it in silence.
In her body,
She holds it.
Carrying it around.
Trying to shed it.
Hiding it from the world,
As she tries to release it.
Releasing it on her own,
Because this is what she does.
She is a healer.
This is her gift.
God gave her darkness,
Because he knew she could carry it.
Carry it while healing.
Healing her world.
Healing each heart.
Each heart she touches.
Holding space for their pain.
Because she can hold it.
She can hold their pain,
Because she can understand it.
She can understand it,
Because she carries it.
She carries her own pain,
As she alchemizes it.
She turns her darkness.
Her darkness into light.
She turns her light.
Her light into love.
She is this beautiful healer.

---

Who knows darkness.
She will hold your hand and walk you…
Walk you through yours.

## Loving Your Soul

Let go of the conditioning.
Let go of what you know.
Let go of the comfort.
The familiar.
Walking into the unknown,
Walk away from insanity.
Walk into peace.
Create your own happiness.
Let yourself see.
See the reality.
See what is real.
Create new beliefs.
Know your value.
Set yourself free,
As you leave the delusion.
The illusion.
The denial.
Give yourself this.
Let your tears fall.
Fall from your eyes.
Set yourself up,
For your new life.
Let your old self go,
As you release the pain.
Acknowledge it all.
Feel your grief.
This is when love enters,
Through the cracks.
Make space for the light.
This is a rebirth.

---

Shedding the old.
Making room for new.
Sitting in your cocoon.
Loving your soul.

# I Know It Wasn't Right

The way they treated me...
I know it wasn't right.
I know it wasn't their fault.
I know where it came from.
They were in pain.
I could feel their pain.
I knew it wasn't right...
How they treated me.
I know they were in pain,
And still...
I allowed it.
I allowed them to belittle me.
I allowed them to walk all over me.
I allowed them to stomp on me.
I knew it wasn't their fault...
But it still does not make it right.
It never had anything to do with me.
Their words.
Their choices.
The way they treated me,
It never had to do with me.
It was their pain.
Never my pain.
It was their fault.
It was never my fault.
I was beautiful underneath it all.
Underneath my pain.
Beauty.
My beauty within.
My light.

My heart.
My soul.
My love.
My light couldn't shine,
While they were around.
Trying to hold them up.
Trying to hold their pain.
Trying to put them before me.
This is what my parents taught me.
Trying to hold their pain,
While I put mine aside.
Trying to help them,
While they abused me.
Trying to love them,
While they chose not to love me.
Trying to respect them,
While they disrespected me.
It was their pain.
It always was.
It was their pain.
It was never my pain.
It was never my fault.
I know this now.
Still pointing the finger.
The finger at me.
Blaming me still,
To avoid their pain.
Blaming me still,
While I learn a new way.
I had to disappear,
To learn new ways.
I had to disappear,

To form a new path.
I am the bad one,
So they say.
I was never the bad one.
I believe this now.
It was their pain.
It was them.
It was never me.
I certainly was not perfect...
But I was never accepted for just being me.
My voice was not heard,
Over and over.
Playing my role...
This was how I was accepted.
Rebelling against control...
The way I was raised.
Just craving nurture...
Please get me out of this cage.
I have learned this,
As I walked away.
I have learned this,
On my new path.
I have learned this,
When I disappeared.
Learning new ways,
So that I could change.
Something they never did.
They did what they knew.
They tried their best...
They did what they could.
I accept this...
It still doesn't make it right.

---

Brought up to self-sacrifice.
Sacrifice my whole being.
Sacrifice my needs.
Sacrifice my feelings.
Sacrifice myself.
Sacrifice it all...
Putting myself last.
Go out on a limb,
To get hurt again.
Trying to save them,
Without saving myself.
Putting them first,
While I put myself last.
I know the way I was treated...
It was not right.
I know the way I should have been treated.
I showed myself this.
Never again,
Will I allow myself to be treated this way again.

# I Gave Myself This

Breathe in.
Breathe out.
That old world.
The chaos.
It's loud.
The noise.
The insanity.
The low frequency.
Such a low vibration...
It was making me sick.
Get me out of here...
Looking back,
With tears in my eyes.
Leaving them all behind.
Behind in that world.
Leaving the noise,
As I take a breath in.
Walking away,
Into silence.
This beautiful peace.
I gave myself this.
Leaving what I knew...
Leaving it behind.
My old world cost me,
Everything I knew.
Letting it go,
To take this breath in.
Breathe in.
Breathe out.
This is peace.

---

Leaving the insanity.
Trading it in for serenity.
This quiet silence.
Breathe in.
Breathe out.
I gave myself this.
My gift to myself.
What a beautiful gift...
I owe this to myself.
Almost forty years surrounded with noise.
Trying to find peace inside of the noise.
Trying to rearrange.
Trying to change.
Trying to fix.
Trying and trying...
Until I had nothing left.
I had nothing left to give...
I needed to rest.
I had nothing left to say...
I needed my rest.
I gave myself this.
This beautiful rest.
This beautiful silence.
This beautiful stillness.
I gave myself this.

## Forget Me

You are going to forget me.
You will forget my face.
You will forget my name.
You will forget all of our memories.
You will forget our good times.
You won't remember.
You are going to forget.
You will forget everything,
But I will still be here.
I will be here to remember.
Remember it all.
I will be here to remember.
Remember your downfall.
We spent hours on the phone.
Talking everyday.
I told you my everything.
I told you all my pain.
I told you every single story,
That ever happened to me.
Just for you to forget.
Forget all about me.
You will forget my name.
You will forget my face.
You will forget that I am your daughter.
You will forget about our phone calls.
You will forget when you came in for haircuts.
You will forget holding me when I was born.
You will forget my birthday parties.
You will forget the day I got married.
You will forget me as a child.

You will forget me as an adult.
You will forget...
But I will remember.
I am feeling this pain.
This pain that caused you to forget.
I am doing this for our family.
I am doing this for me.
I am doing this for my body.
I am doing this so that I won't forget.
I won't forget,
Just as you did.
I am breaking this cycle.
You will forget,
But I will not.
I am here to remember.
I remember,
And I won't forget.
You will forget me,
But I won't forget you.

## This Is Why You Are Here

The pain you feel,
As you break the cycle.
The tears you will cry,
As you leave behind.
People you love.
People you know.
The anger that arises,
As you realize.
The way you were treated,
Was not right.
The way you were raised...
To self-sacrifice.
Put yourself last.
Put them first.
Do not use your voice.
Do not speak up.
Shove everything under the rug.
Shove it all down.
Until it builds up.
Emotional suppression,
Is what you were taught.
Hide your pain.
Shove it away.
Shove the emotions down.
Until an illness shows up.
Shove it away...
For another day.
Another day passes...
Keep shoving it away.
Do not deal with anything.

Push it down.
Make everyone happy.
Please them and please them.
Abandon yourself.
Wear a mask,
Your whole life.
Play pretend.
You must self-sacrifice.
Breaking this cycle,
Is putting yourself first.
Show up and be you,
No matter what.
Breaking the cycle,
Is speaking up.
Speaking your truth...
Being you...
Every single time.
If it bothers you,
Say it.
You always say it.
Speak it and say it.
Always say it.
Stand up for yourself,
No matter who it upsets.
Walk away from abuse.
Do not allow yourself to be used.
You are not an object.
You do not play a game.
You are this beautiful person,
Who was made.
You did not choose to be here.
But you choose now.

Make a new choice.
You choose every single time.
Listen to your intuition.
Lose your conditioning.
Follow your gut.
Be honest.
Be authentic.
Be genuine,
And vulnerable.
Share your story.
Lose the fear.
Embrace being open.
This is why you are here.
Your purpose.
You have found it.
You are now sharing it with the world.
It is okay if they don't like you.
That is their problem,
Not yours.
Keep being you.
Keep being authentic.
Keep sharing your love,
And listen to your heart.
Understand that this...
Is why you are here.

## This Is Who You Always Have Been

The slowness.
The silence.
The serenity.
The bliss.
The solitude.
The stillness.
The love.
The beauty.
The tranquility.
The divinity.
It's lovely.
It's vibrant.
It's quiet.
It's peaceful.
It is still.
Inside of the chaos.
Find your peace,
Inside of the mess.
Breathe in.
Breathe out.
Inside of the storm.
Be in it.
It won't last forever.
It will pass.
Let it all come.
Let it all go.
Let it all be.
Let it all leave.
This is not you.
It is time to release.

Release and let go.
It is time to breathe.
It is time to rest.
Nothing to do.
Nowhere to be.
This day is for you.
Stay true.
Stay true to yourself.
Whatever you need.
Just breathe.
Breathe in.
Breathe out.
Just be still.
This is you.
Holding your worth.
Holding your love.
Holding your light.
Let it shine bright.
This is you.
This is your truth.
Sitting in the storms,
Seeing it all.
Feeling it all.
Releasing it all.
Acceptance and forgiveness.
The darkness.
The hardness.
The radiance.
The vibrance.
The silence.
The stillness.
It is all worth it.

---

Because at the end,
You become you.
Shedding the layers,
Finding you again.
Coming home to yourself.
This is who you are.
This is who you always have been.

## I Set It All Down

Carrying this burden.
Carrying this pain.
Carrying this weight.
This trauma,
Only I know.
Carrying this sorrow.
Carrying this betrayal.
Carrying around this burden.
This burden,
I will put down.
It is weighing me down.
Keeping me glued down.
What I saw.
What I experienced.
The people who were supposed to love me,
Were covered in pain.
It never had to do with me,
It was their pain.
It was not my pain.
Carrying around this love for them.
Carrying around expectations of them.
Carrying around this plan in my head.
Carrying around this future I planned.
This future,
I must let go.
This vision.
This expectation.
This beautiful picture I painted.
I will put this all down.
I set it down.

I set this down now.
I cannot carry it...
Not anymore.
I didn't want it to be this.
But I will accept this.
It is this way.
I accept this now.
This reality.
I accept this.
I must walk away,
And leave this burden to stay.
Walking away.
I just cannot stay.
This illusion I lived in.
This pretty picture I painted.
Seeing the best.
Loving so big.
Brushing everything to the side.
Playing pretend.
Shoving everything away.
Trying to stay.
Trying to hold on,
So that I won't feel this pain.
This pain of detachment.
Detaching from what I know.
Everything I knew.
Everything I loved...
It is all gone.
I set it all down.
It was weighing me down.
Holding me back.
Reaching for me.

Trying to get me to stay.
Stay where I was.
Trying to get me to be.
Be who I used to be.
I am not her anymore.
I lay her down at my feet,
As I get on my knees.
I get on my knees,
Because I am so weak.
Filled up with grief.
As I lay it all down.
I am on my knees,
As I surrender to peace.
I lay it all down.
I set it all down,
As I feel it all leave.

# I Didn't Want To See

I didn't know what I know.
What I know now.
I didn't want to see.
I didn't want to believe.
Believe that my parents...
Put themselves before me.
I wanted to believe they were great.
That they were perfect...
But that is not the case.
They are imperfect and flawed...
Just like me.
I didn't want to see.
That I was tossed to the side.
Punished to the extreme.
Taught to believe,
Anything they say.
Let them manipulate me.
Let them punish me,
And demean me.
Dismiss my voice.
Shove me to the side,
As they walk on me.
Pretend to be...
Who they wanted me to be.
Be quiet and stay small.
Put my feelings to the side,
As I ignore it all.
Ignore what was going on.
Ignore was the way.
Shoving it all away.

Be happy all the time.
Smile!! It's fine!!
Continue my life,
Like nothing is wrong.
This is the way,
I was brought up.
I allowed this...
And allowed this.
Until the day I stopped.
Until the day I put my foot down.
Until the day...
The day I walked away.
Walked away for good.
I will not allow this...
Not anymore.
I couldn't see.
I didn't want to believe.
Wearing rose-colored glasses,
For years and years.
Living with an illusion.
Living in a delusion.
I didn't want to see.
See the reality.
The reality of my parents...
That they never healed.
Then they had me...
And I was thrown into their mess.
Thrown into their wounds.
Thrown into their rules,
That they made from their pain.
They built a life with their trauma.
This beautiful illusion,

Without real conversation.
Without realizing the truth.
They didn't want to see,
So they turned it on me.
It was easier for them,
To paint me as the bad one.
I was the problem.
I was the reason.
The reason for their turmoil.
The reason for their chaos.
It was easier for them,
To paint me as their scapegoat.
Rather than go inside.
Inside of themselves.
To look at their pain.
To feel their pain.
It was easier to see...
Me as that problem.
But it was never me...
It was never, ever me.
I was brought into,
Their distorted reality.
That they didn't heal from.
They still have no idea,
Where that pain even came from.
They think it was me.
It is easier this way.
Easier for them,
To believe it was me.
It was never me...
I believe this wholeheartedly.
I believe this, finally.

I was born into pain.
I poured my heart into them.
Without seeing the truth.
I poured my heart into them,
Just to have them throw me away.
This pain in my heart,
That I live with everyday.
This betrayal,
That I feel.
But maybe it was never a betrayal…
It was that they couldn't see.
They just couldn't see.
See their own pain.
They would rather blame me.
It is easiest this way.
Easiest for them.
I will continue to grieve…
As I let them be.

## Something To See

Once you see,
You cannot unsee.
And I see.
I see now.
I see the mess.
I see the chaos.
I see this lack of accountability.
I see when they do not take responsibility.
I appreciate vulnerability.
I love integrity.
I see the masks.
I see the facades.
I see the illusion...
All the delusion.
I understand now,
Why it is this way.
I understand now...
That everyone just sees...
What they want to see.
It is easier that way.
That they see how they want to see.
Painting a picture.
This pretty, little picture.
Painting a picture,
Of whatever reality you desire.
Choosing to see,
What you want to see.
Choosing to see,
What is easier to see.
Choosing to see,

And you cannot unsee.
The illusion is gone.
The pretty little picture,
Is put down.
I have put it away.
Put it away for good.
The reality is known.
The distortion is gone.
This is the reality.
The mess.
The chaos.
The goodness.
The hardship.
The love.
The fights.
The emotions.
The light.
The darkness.
It all comes and it all goes.
Let it all pass.
Let it all leave.
But this is the reality.
This is the truth.
This is how it is.
The rose-colored glasses have come off.
The waves of emotion.
The tears that flow.
The rest that is needed,
When you realize the truth.
The silence and serenity.
Leaving the noise,
To sit in this tranquility.

Nothing to do.
Nowhere to go.
Just something to see.
And once you see,
You cannot unsee.

# I Am Here Now

It was me the whole time.
The one who couldn't see.
It was me trying to get out.
It was me trying to leave.
It was me who betrayed me.
It was me who became who they wanted me to be.
Here is me...
Taking accountability.
I am taking responsibility.
It was me who showed up...
Just to please them.
It was me who stayed silent.
It was me who stayed small.
It was me who stayed controlled.
It was me who couldn't see.
I couldn't see me...
My beautiful soul.
I couldn't see me...
How I showed up.
I couldn't see me.
I didn't value me.
I allowed mistreatment.
I allowed disrespect.
I couldn't see me.
Now I need to forgive me.
Forgive myself.
Forgive my heart.
Forgive my love.
The love I gave out.
Forgive my light.

---

The light I turned off.
Forgive my soul.
My soul that I hid.
The parts of me that I hid away.
The parts of me that I didn't appreciate.
The parts of me that I buried deep.
The parts of me that I left behind.
The parts of me that I did not show.
The parts of me that had so much sorrow.
I didn't hold them,
Like they needed to be held.
I didn't love them,
Like they needed to be loved.
I didn't show up,
The way they needed me to show up.
I am here now,
To give them what they need.
I am here now,
To speak up when it is time.
I am here now,
To leave when it is time to leave.
I am here now,
To rest when it is time to rest.
I am here now,
When it is time to see.
I am here now.
I always will be.
I am here now...
To set myself free.

# I Expect The Same From You

We all have it.
Pain inside.
We all have it.
The hurt inside.
We all have it.
The visions we remember.
The tears we need to let go of.
We all have it.
Hearts that have been broken.
We all have it.
Childhood trauma.
Every single one of us.
We are all the same.
We are all connected.
We are all one.
I will understand you.
But I will not allow you to...
Project your pain onto me.
Stab me in my heart,
Just because you hurt.
I will not allow you to disrespect me.
I will not allow you to stomp all over me.
I will not allow you to paint a picture.
A picture that is distorted,
Just to make you smile.
I will not allow you to ostracize me.
Just because you can't look at your own pain.
I will not allow you,
To silence my voice.
I have pain too,

---

That I keep inside.
I carry it around.
It is buried deep inside.
I have hurt too,
That I don't put onto you.
I have broken pieces,
That I have been mending back together.
I take my pain,
And I hold it for myself.
I know it is my own pain...
To carry and to hold.
I know that my pain,
Does not belong to you.
I will carry my pain,
As I release each piece.
I release it in silence.
It is no one else's.
This is my pain...
I expect the same from you.
I will walk away,
If you try to give me your pain.
Throw it onto me,
Because you don't want to see.
I will walk away,
Because I have one expectation of you.
That you hold your pain...
Just like I am holding mine.
That pain is yours to hold.
Your burden to carry.
Your pain is yours,
That you keep buried.
That is yours to feel.

It is not mine to hold.
I will give it back....
Right back to you.
If you even try to give it to me...
I will walk away.
No that is not mine.
That is yours.
No that is not mine.
This is mine.
I will carry mine,
As you carry yours.
I will help you carry yours,
As you help me carry mine.
But I cannot be the only one,
Carrying everything.
I cannot be the only one...
The only one who sees.
I cannot be the only one,
Putting in the work.
I cannot be the only one,
To carry all your pain.
I take my power back,
As I separate myself.
As I take my pain and feel it,
And give yours back to you.
This was never mine to hold.
This was never mine to feel.
This was never my job...
...The scapegoat...
It was just a role.
A role that I took on.
This role,

I end now.
This was never who I was.
I never knew who I was...
Because I was too busy playing this role.
The role as your scapegoat.
I end this role for good now,
As I hand your pain back to you.
I am done carrying it...
I can no longer hold it.
I set it all down...
This generational pain,
That I have carried.
I will feel mine,
As you feel yours.
I will feel mine...
And I expect the same from you.

## Isn't It Ironic?

Rebuild and replace.
Reconstruct piece by piece.
Putting it all back together again.
Servicing my heart.
Exactly what it needs.
*What do you need?*
A question I will ask.
I ask myself this.
Every single day.
*I just need to be taken care of...*
The answer for today.
Rest and relax.
Recharge and self-care.
Feel this sadness,
That is here.
Sit in it.
Cry the tears.
Feel the pain.
So that it will pass.
You are not alone.
Because you have me.
This self-love thing...
Is where I am at.
Beautiful surrender.
Silence and quiet.
I finally hear my voice,
That was covered for years.
Covered with noise.
It is now loud and clear.
This intuition.

---

It is real.
This is me.
My pain.
My trauma,
I will release.
Piece by piece,
It leaves me.
Piece by piece,
I release.
Self-love.
Self-worth.
I found my light.
I now know,
I deserved to be treated right.
I now understand.
It was never me.
I just carried their pain,
So they wouldn't have to.
I took it and took it,
Until I didn't.
I held it.
I carried it.
Until I stopped.
I did it all...
I did it for them.
I did it because I cared.
I did it because I loved.
But I had to stop.
I was stomped on enough.
I was done being used.
I was done being needed,
To pick them back up.

Pick up all the pieces.
The pieces for them.
I picked up their pieces,
When I had all of my pieces.
I was done giving out tools.
I was done being thrown away.
Tossed to the side.
Expecting me to self-sacrifice.
Sacrifice myself.
One more time.
Only one more time.
Once more...
Again.
I was all set with that.
I was done having their emotions thrown at me.
Projecting what they don't want to see...
Putting it all on me.
I was done with zero accountability.
I was done not having them take any responsibility.
Always being the one to forgive and forget.
Sweeping it all under the rug.
Pretend that it's fine...
Smile all the time.
I was done being the one,
To put it back together.
I was done being the fixer.
The mender.
The forgiver.
The doer.
The caretaker.
I was done putting myself aside.
Just one more time.

---

Forgive and forget...
That's how they roll.
Nothing is discussed.
Just give it some time.
It will all be better...
With just a little time.
Time we don't have...
Because time is being taken.
Everything on their end...
Is being taken.
Forgotten.
Everything will be forgotten.
Isn't it ironic?
The pain I feel.
The pain I shoved down...
It all will be forgotten.
Where it came from.
The root cause.
It will all be forgotten.
I am to blame...
He will take that to his grave.
Instead of knowing the truth.
Seeing the truth.
Feeling the truth.
This is my role.
To carry this burden...
It is my job to feel it.
The cycle breaker.
The black sheep.
The transitional character.
The villain.
The one who speaks up.

Speaks up with the truth.
Who carries all the pain,
From all of the abuse.
The abuse that will be forgotten...
Isn't it ironic?

## ...As You Walk Into Stillness...

Slowness.
Stillness.
Serenity.
Silence.
Sensations.
Emotions.
My breath.
Breathe in.
Breathe out.
My peace.
My light.
My love.
My soul.
Beautiful surrender.
Inside of this stillness.
Quiet the chaos.
The noise of the world.
Societal expectations.
Societal beliefs.
I surrender,
Into me.
This is who I am,
Underneath it all.
This is who I am,
Without the competition.
The competition of the world.
The next new edition...
Of who you are now.
The new rendition...
Of who you must become.

Become who they want you to be.
Fit into society.
Deal with the insanity.
Compete with humanity.
...so radically.
...so drastically.
Either this way or that way.
Agree with this mentality.
This societal conditioning.
Instant gratification.
Suffocation.
Inside of the insanity.
The chaos.
The norm.
What fits.
The masks.
The facades.
Put it all down...
As you walk into stillness.
Into silence.
Into love.

## So Rooted

Become so rooted.
Rooted in who you are.
Rooted in your beliefs.
Rooted to your heart.
Become so rooted...
Nothing can affect it.
The outside world doesn't matter.
Stay grounded in who you are.
Know yourself so well,
That no one else can pull you down.
Stay inside of stillness,
Until it is time to come out.
Stay grounded in yourself.
You know yourself well.
You know your intuition.
You know this sensation.
You know this voice.
This voice within you.
Only you know this.
Only you hear this.
Be so connected.
Connected to your breath.
Be in this moment.
This moment is all you have left.
Another moment passes.
Onto the next.
You stay inside of presence.
Another emotion arises,
For you to release.
Another tear drops.

Drops from your eyes.
Another lesson comes.
Comes for you to learn.
Your lessons and tools.
You carry with you.
You have collected them all,
Do not put them down,
Clarity is here.
Serenity is near.
You have dropped your fear.
Your intuition is so clear.
Another moment is here.
This time it is joy.
It is fleeting.
It comes,
And then it leaves.
Along with everything else.
Let it all come.
Let it all leave.
Take your breath in...
Embrace your dreams.

# The Shift In The Air

Feeling the shift.
This shift in the air.
Feeling the shift.
This shift in your heart.
Feeling this shift.
This brokenness,
That comes when you decide.
To leave everything behind.
Feeling the grief,
For yourself.
Your life you lived…
Your whole life.
Feeling this grief,
As you decide.
To leave the life you built.
You are leaving it behind.
Beautiful people,
That you loved so much.
Knowing they can't come,
To where you are going.
They don't understand.
They are trying to pull you back.
Where is she?
We need her.
Where did she go?
Waiting for clarity,
Making this decision.
Waiting alone,
Listening to your voice.
It will come.

With patience,
You sit.
You are waiting,
For clarity to come.
Leaving behind,
A life you loved.
A life you built.
A you that you made.
You made this you,
And now you must let her go.
She kept you safe,
When you had nothing left.
When everything was taken.
When everything crumbled.
She knew what to do,
Every single time.
She knew the right move,
When nothing made sense.
She was strong and resilient.
She kept moving and going...
She lived in her masculine,
She had forgotten about her feminine.
She had shoved her feminine so far down...
She was never accepted,
Or wanted around.
She shoved her femininity...
She shoved it away.
Until the day,
You let her back in.
You found her.
You loved her.
You had never even met her.

---

She was loved,
And admired.
She was adored,
And held.
No more hiding,
She was herself.
She chose herself,
Each and every time.
Balancing her masculine,
And feminine side.
Letting go of her pain.
Grieving it all.
Embracing this shift.
This shift in the air.

## Unreachable

She is unreachable.
She is not figure-out-able,
As she becomes vulnerable.
She is unpredictable.
She is indescribable.
She is impossible...
Impossible to understand.
She doesn't make sense.
She doesn't fit into a box.
Orderly.
Just so....
Prim and proper...
"You must stay here."
Perfectly aligned...
"Don't move."
"Don't grow."
Words she has been told.
Words she doesn't listen to.
Words she shrugs off,
As she forms a new path.
Letting it all go,
Taking off the masks.
Taking off the masks,
She was told to wear.
Taking off her armor to protect her heart.
Stripping herself down.
Right down to her soul.
Her bare-naked self.
Naked and whole.
Without any walls.

Shrugging of the words.
The words she has been told.
"You must be this girl."
"You must be her."
Words that don't matter....
Words that don't make sense.
"Stay the same."
No way.
Not a chance.
Keep moving.
It is a new day.
A new day to be different...
She will never remain the same.
Her spirit is free.
Her light that shines.
She can't be told.
Told what to do.
She can't be controlled.
She can't be kept on a leash.
She cannot be given a script.
She needs to feel free.
Free and different...
She doesn't fit into society.
She is different than the rest.
Different than the crowd.
She goes against the grain.
She will never fit in.
She is who she is.
She will say what she wants to say.
She will never remain the same...
So move aside,
As she commits.

Commits to change.
Commits to herself.
Commits to her soul,
As she leaves the façade.
The illusion,
And the masks.
She leaves it all behind…
As she creates her own path.

# Letting Go Of Hope

Letting go of hope,
Is letting it just be.
Not having an answer.
Being in full surrender.
Letting go of the expectation,
To just be in the moment.
Letting go of what you want it to be.
Letting go of what you wish it could be.
Letting go of the old me...
As I sit here,
Blissfully.
I literally...
Have no energy.
The grief has washed over me.
As I let go of everything.
Every goal.
Every dream.
That hope that I held.
That hope that I carried.
That hope weighed me down.
The denial.
The illusion.
The false perception.
The daydreams,
That came with expectations.
Expectations of what I want it to be.
"But I want this...
And I want that...
I want it to look this way...
And I want it to go this way.

I want it to be this.
I don't want it be that.
This is what I want..."
And this was the hope.
The hope that I held.
The hope that weighed me down.
This hope is not life.
This hope is not real.
What is real is this moment,
As I let hope fall away.
What is real is who I am.
Who I am,
Without this hope.
Who I am,
Deep inside.
Who I am.
Who I really am.
My heart.
Who am I?
Just me.
Who am I?
As I just let myself be.
Who am I?
As I surrender.
Surrender into faith.
Surrender without the hope.
Letting go of the hope...
And just trusting in each moment.
Each moment that comes.
Each moment that arises.
Each moment that passes.
Let go of the hope.

---

It is not mine to carry.
Set it all down.
Surrender to the ground.
Surrender to the earth,
And set myself free.
Surrender to my hope...
It is the only way...
To just be.

## Those Voices Of Fear

Those voices of fear.
Holding you back.
Those voices of your mind.
They are not real.
Limiting beliefs...
Holding you back.
They come to take you over.
They come to hold you back.
Those voices that you hear...
Those voices of fear.
Those voices are not you.
They are not who you are.
*You must be successful.*
*You must be this.*
*You must be that.*
*It must look this way...*
*For it to work.*
*You must continue...*
*The same way you have.*
*Stay the same.*
*Stay in the known.*
*Stay in the familiar.*
*Do not go into the unknown.*
These are the voices.
That will keep you held back.
These are the voices,
That keep you closed.
Lose this belief.
Lose it now...
This is not who you are...

It is just a belief.
These voices come.
They come as fear.
Disguised as you…
But this is not you at all.
These voices.
This fear.
They want it to make sense.
Fit in a box.
*Do it this way.*
*Just like this.*
*Have this picture painted…*
*This pretty little picture.*
*It all must make sense.*
*Do it like this.*
Jealousy and envy…
This will keep you small.
Pride and hate…
Will keep you held back.
Let the darkness go.
Let it all go.
Let it all out.
Let it all leave.
This leaves a space.
A space for light.
Let the light in,
And open your heart.
Those voices shut off.
Because love is the answer…
It always has been.
Love and acceptance.
Surrender and faith.

Beautiful forgiveness is where you will be.
Silence and serenity...
Oh,
That beauty.

## Just Be

Just Be.
Just sit.
Nothing to do.
Nowhere to go.
Just be.
Right here.
In this moment.
Presence,
And stillness.
This beautiful moment.
Silence,
And grieving.
This grief arises.
Loss and change.
So unexpected.
Just let it all be.

## Those Colors Of The Sky

Those colors of the sky.
Each one,
It's own hue.
Each one...
Blended perfectly.
Each one,
Representing you.
In each moment that passes.
A new color that moves.
A new color that blends.
Blends in with the clouds.
Blending with the oranges.
Turning into red.
Turning into blue.
Such a beautiful hue.
Each color moves.
Never staying the same.
A different day.
A different hue.
This beautiful you.
Changing with the sunset.
Rising with the sun.
Trusting in the unknown.
What color is next?
Beautiful reds.
Beautiful pinks.
Those bright yellows.
Blues and purples.
Changing with the wind.
Changing with time.

---

Never committing to the same.
The same old hue.
Blending and changing.
You are not that same old you.
Just like the sky.
The colors of the sky.
They are never the same.
The same sky you knew.
A different sky each night.
A different sky with each sunrise.
You are never the same,
Just like the sky.
You are never the same,
With each sunrise.
You become new,
With each sunset.
A beautiful you.
Each color of the sky.
This is you.
You get to choose.
The reds.
The yellows.
The blues.
Whichever way the wind blows.
Wherever your light shines.
Wherever the clouds are.
These colors of the sky.
The sunset.
The sunrise.
This becomes your story.
Because with each moment that passes,
The sky is your glory.

Each color that changes.
These are your phases.
Never staying the same...
Always committing to change.
Just like these colors of the sky...
Constantly changing on the inside.
Surrender to this...
In this moment.
The colors of the sky...
They are you.
Blissfully radiant.
Peaceful and vibrant.
Colorful in silence.
Trusting in your guidance.
This moment is priceless.
Imperfectly flawless.
The colors of the sky are limitless.
Just as you are...
This beautiful you.

## It Just Is... What It Is.

Lose the outcome.
The outcome.
The ending.
The control.
The certainty.
Lose the expectation of what you want it to be.
Just let it be.
Whatever it wants to be.
Let it be.
However it ends up...
Is how it is supposed to be.
Let it go.
The fantasy.
The denial.
The illusion.
The delusion.
Be in the reality.
This is the actuality.
...you are free...
Free from what you thought it would be.
The way things ended up,
Are not what you actually dreamed.
You thought you could predict.
You thought you knew.
You thought you could pick.
You thought you had control.
But you never did.
It was just a picture.
This pretty little picture.
This picture you painted.

That you thought you could live.
But this was the wrong way.
This path that you picked.
It wasn't what you thought.
Let go of it.
Let everything be.
Let it all just be.
Let it continue to be,
Whatever it wants to be.
You will be free...
When you set it all down.
When you surrender,
And just let it be.
When you choose acceptance.
Acceptance and reality.
Let go of the fantasy.
This is the actuality.
Sitting in uncertainty.
Letting go of predictability.
Life is a mystery.
A mystery of moments...
That you must let be.
Let it play out,
Just as it should.
The disappointments.
The grief.
Those beautiful moments,
That last just a second.
That we want to hold onto.
Those beautiful moments are fleeting...
Be in the moments.
Be so in the moment,

That you forget to take the picture.
You forget why you are there...
You get lost in the moment.
Your heart,
It opens.
At that very moment.
Your gratitude is explosive,
In this very moment.
Because the moments you had to let go of,
That brought you to this moment.
The love that filled you up,
It doesn't last forever.
Soak up each moment.
Soak up the love.
Soak up the beauty.
The beauty in each moment.
Let go of control.
You cannot control it.
You must master letting it flow.
Letting it be.
Everything the way it should be.
Let it play out,
Just as it should.
Open your heart.
Accept the unknown.
Sit in the uncertainty,
As you realize life's mystery.
Trust in your spirituality.
You have no control...
You never did.
Surrender to this.
Surrender to your breath.

Let your heart lead.
Let go of speed.
Embracing being slow,
To take it all in.
Enjoy this very moment.
This is where it begins.
The start of the next moment.
Begin again.
Onto the next.
Take it all in.
You can't get it back,
As you keep letting go.
You must learn to let go.
You are not in control.
Let it all go.
Let it be slow.
There is no rush.
Right here.
Right now.
It just is...
What it is.

## This Place Of Love

That plan.
The plan you had.
The plan you had did not go...
As you planned.
Everything you wished for...
Everything you loved...
You had to set it all down.
You had to walk away.
You had to surrender.
Surrender to your plan.
This plan that you had...
It wasn't set in stone.
This dream in your head...
It was out of your control.
This pretty little picture...
It had to be taken down.
This fantasy.
This illusion.
The way you wanted it to be.
The people you loved.
The people you hugged.
The people you held closest to you.
You had to grieve them,
As you set them down.
Took them off their pedestal.
You had them on this pedestal.
The men in your life...
You held them so high.
You looked up to them,
Because you wanted to believe.

Believe they would save you.
Keep you safe,
And guide you.
You looked to them for direction.
You trusted in them.
A whole piece of your heart,
You had given to them.
They took it for them.
You were left with this void.
Pieces of your heart...
Completely destroyed.
You gave it to them.
Putting your faith into them.
Instead of trusting yourself.
And what you knew to be true.
It was never you...
It was them the whole time.
They were not whole,
So they took from you.
Because you filled them up.
Because you loved them so much.
You gave your heart to them.
And left yourself broken.
Frozen.
You left yourself empty.
You sacrificed yourself...
You did it for them.
You believed in them.
You had love for them.
You had to repair...
Pick up each piece.
Give yourself the love,

That you gave away.
So freely...
Your love...
You gave it away.
Leaving nothing for yourself,
As you laid on the ground.
And couldn't get up...
Filled up with grief.
Sadness and sorrow.
Heaviness.
The weight.
This weight you carried.
You have put it all down.
You will not carry it.
You put it all down,
As you walk away.
Protecting your heart.
You stopped playing the games.
Respecting yourself.
Respecting your heart.
Your heart.
Your wholeness.
This is yours now.
You will not give it away.
You have earned this place.
This place of freedom.
This place of love.

## Life Blooms

But life does not bloom...
Through control.
Through certainty.
Through envy.
Through compassion.
Through jealousy.
Through perfection.
Through expectation.
Through judgment.
Through knowing it all.

Life blooms through...
Losing it all.
The pain.
The truth.
The grief.
The risks.
The unraveling.
The stillness.
The darkness.
The undoing.
The loneliness.
The creating.
Making mistakes and failing.
Praying.
Adventure.
Wonder.
Chaos.
Confusion.
Curiosity.

Uncertainty.
Spontaneity.
Mystery,

With patience.
With slowness.
Stillness and solitude.
Consideration and observation.
Trust and surrender.
Letting go and living.
Feeling and releasing.
Reflecting and crying.
Falling and rising.
Healing and grieving.
Reflecting and learning.
Growing and changing.
Smiling and laughing.
Having gratitude and thanking.
Wanting nothing and giving.
Resting and relaxing.
Compassion and understanding.
Acceptance and forgiving.
Choosing and praying.
Silently waiting.
Pausing and appreciating.
Manifesting and believing.
Apologizing and acknowledging.
Moving and dancing.
Writing and singing.
Detachment and unplugging.
Caring and connecting.
Soul embracing.

Challenge facing.
Responding vs. reacting.
Hearing and seeing.
Smelling and touching.
Forgetting and remembering.
Imperfectly admitting.
Peacefully enjoying.
Living in the moment.
Leaning in and loving.
Loving fully.

Blooming.
Becoming.
Breathing.
Balancing.
Being.
Bravery.
Beauty.
Brightly.
Blissfully.
Believing.
Brilliantly
Breathtaking.

This is everlasting.
So ravishing.
So completely stunning.
This path.
This journey.
This incomplete masterpiece.

# Imagine This World

Imagine this world.
A world wrapped in kindness.
A world that gives compassion...
No matter what.
This world that knows love.
All it knows is love.
Unconditional love.
A world that shows up.
A world that shines bright.
Just a high vibrational world.
That doesn't have wounds.
That only has high value.
So mystical.
So magical.
So radiant and ravishing.
So beautiful.
So brilliant.
Absolutely magnificent.
So connected.
Connected with love.
We are all one.
No projections,
Or arguments.
No judgement or blame.
Disagreements are okay,
And completely accepted.
I am allowed to be me.
You are allowed to be you.
There is no hate here.
Here in this world.

There is only love here.
Putting down the fear.
Putting away the envy.
The jealousy.
The pride and apathy.
Those low vibrations that are being thrown around.
People emptying themselves out...
Throwing this out into the world,
So they don't have to feel.
Putting it out into the world...
This world that we live in,
It doesn't have to be this.
Why is it like this?
Staying away from the mess.
The insanity.
The chaos.
Building my own little world.
My own world of love.
My world of being.
Being who you are.
Not becoming who you are told to be.
Not becoming what fits into society,
So you can fit in.
Stand out...
It's okay.
It is my own little world now.
I left my old world.
I left it behind.
This world of separation.
This world of suppression.
The world of instant gratification.
This world of facades,

Where everyone wore masks.
This world of ego.
I have left it behind,
To create what is mine.
This world is mine.
The world of love.
Imagine this world.

## She Changed Her Story

She changed her story,
Just like that.
She changed her ending.
She changed her traditions.
She changed her life.
She changed what she put up with.
She changed her worth.
She changed her heart.
She made a new start,
By letting go of it all.
Everything she loved.
Everything is gone.
Everything she knew,
Is in the past.
In the rearview...
She is not looking back.
She made a decision,
For herself.
She made the choice,
To not abandon herself.
She chose a direction.
She walked away from self-sacrifice.
She made the decision,
To rise from her fall.
Her fall.
Her demise.
She shut her eyes.
...One more time.
She prayed for her new life,
As tears fell from her eyes.

Her heart shattered,
One more time.
Never again would she accept,
Anything less.
Nothing but the best.
Walking away...
From disrespect,
And cruelty.
From manipulation...
And bullies.
Towards beauty and serenity.
Lovely tranquility.
Compassion and understanding.
Walking away from black or white.
Moving straight into the grey.
So many options.
So many choices.
It could go this way,
Or that way.
Her way,
Or their way.
Making her own path...
Being so unsure of which way to go...
Does she stay or go?
Is it now or later?
She will listen to herself.
She will trust herself.
She will make the choice,
As she listens to her own voice.
Her voice that was shoved away,
For so many years.
Her voice that was not heard,

So many times.
Her voice that was dismissed,
Time after time.
Walking away...
Towards herself.
Towards her heart.
Towards her light.
Towards her life,
That she chose for herself.

## ...As I Blow You This Kiss

When life changes.
When life comes to a screeching halt.
When you are told you will forget everything.
When you are told your life is about to change.
When you lived your life,
For everyone else.
When you realize you worked your life away.
When you realize your memories are not here to stay.
When you realize everything is about to change.
When you realize you have no future.
When you realize your life will stop.
Putting down your hobbies.
Putting away your life.
Setting down your personality.
Turning in your knowledge.
Realizing your world is not the same.
You do not have your future.
The future you had planned out.
One that you will not remember.
You give up all your dreams.
All to dismember.
Dismember your life...
The life that you had laid out.
The life that you really wanted.
The life that will just fizzle away.
All because you will forget...
You will forget the love you shared.
You will forget the memories you made.
You will forget the relationships you built.
You will forget the importance.

The importance of the love you held.
The love that you carried in your heart.
You will forget the close bonds you had.
The bonds you made.
The bonds you shared.
You will forget you and I.
You already have...
I never even got the chance to say goodbye,
Because the you that I knew disappeared.
Quickly changed.
As your insides rearranged.
There was nothing I could do to stop it.
I just had to let you go.
I just had to watch...
Without any control.
As you left.
The you that I knew,
Was no longer here.
I never had the chance,
To tell you goodbye.
Because you shoved me away,
As you stomped on my heart.
You pushed me away...
I could no longer stay.
Because of these games,
That you were being directed to play.
You had no idea...
Because you never had the chance.
To see what I saw.
You never had the chance to remove the illusion.
The illusion you lived in.

The denial you stayed in.
You never had the chance to figure it out...
This diagnosis came,
Before you ever had the chance.
It came to take you away.
The memories you made,
I will carry with me...
I do this for you.
Because no matter what...
I understand you.
I have empathy for you...
And I will do this for you.
I will carry them with me,
As they are taken from you.
I hold them in my heart,
As you wither away.
As you forget who I am...
You will forget my name.
You will never even know...
The pain that I carried.
I never got the chance,
To share it with you.
This diagnosis came...
To take you away.
This diagnosis came.
It came too soon.
It came to take you away...
I am learning now,
To take care of myself.
Without your calls.
Without your love.

Without your guidance.
I am learning to do this...
I am learning how to do this.
I am learning how to let go...
With having you right down the road.
I am learning to grieve,
As you are still here.
I am learning to forgive.
I am learning to understand.
I am learning to live,
As you forget.
I am learning to surrender...
As I remember,
Our memories that we made.
We made them together.
The memories you will forget.
The memories I wanted you to cherish.
This is my job now,
As I learn to let you go.
As I learn to live life without you.
This is all out of my control.
I am allowing you to be...
In the life that you chose.
I will leave you in your life,
As I send you love from my heart.
I send you love every day.
Every morning,
I pray.
That you receive this love...
That it reaches your heart.
I hope that you know,

That I love you no matter what.
But I could no longer subject,
My heart anymore.
I needed to protect myself and my heart.
Something you did not teach me.
Something I had to learn on my own.
I needed to see.
I needed to understand.
This reality.
The reality that was hidden,
Behind all the pain.
That I carried for years.
That was passed down to me.
Generationally,
That we all carried.
This pain that we held...
This pain that was inside.
This self-sacrifice.
As I moved through each layer,
As I released.
I release this for good.
As I now see...
I see the reality.
That you never saw.
It is too late now...
But I am doing this work.
I am doing this for us all.
I am doing this out of love...
You can't even see this,
Because your vision is blurred.
By the illusion and diagnosis.

I understand this.
I set down my anger.
I need to set this down...
As I cry these tears of grief.
I cry them for you.
Each tear that falls from my eyes...
Each one represents my love for you.
Although I am not there with you,
You are in my heart.
I carry this around...
As you forget.
I carry this around...
This pain in my chest.
I carry this around...
As I change my mindset.
As I learn to let you go,
With you right down the road.
I know that you don't know...
Because you never did the work.
You couldn't release the pain,
Because you didn't have the tools.
It was easier to stay,
In the life you knew.
It was easier to stay,
Than it was to change.
I understand this.
I will make sense of all of this.
It doesn't mean it was okay,
But there is nothing I can do now.
It is all out of my control...
As I lay this all down.
I must learn to accept...

---

This is the chapter we are in.
Breaking this cycle...
As you forget.
I still send you love,
As I blow you this kiss.

# You With Your Roots

Be open enough to see.
Be humble enough to fall.
Fall into reality.
Instead of covering yourself up.
Covering yourself in the denial.
Covering yourself up in the illusion.
Hiding away.
Just so you won't see.
You won't see the truth,
That society keeps.
Keeps locked away...
"Society says..."
Take it all away.
It is all fake.
Just because society says...
Does not mean it is this way.
"This is the way..."
Society says.
Just because society says...
Does not mean,
You follow that path.
You are on your own path.
You pave the way...
You stand in your power.
Finally you are there.
You don't need to say anything at all.
Your energy speaks for itself.
You no longer explain.
You no longer defend.
You just let it all go.

---

You let it all be.
It all is what it is.
No need to compete.
Just living your life.
You finally get to be you.
Sending love to the world,
As you stand in your power.
Your true self,
In your truest expression.
Living life to the fullest...
Feeling your emotions.
Allowing this grief to wash over you,
As you cry your tears.
You set it all down,
You have put down your fear,
You have moved through the layers.
Each layer of pain.
Each layer has a story.
A story you have heard.
You heard it in silence,
That you gave to yourself.
You listened to it all...
You listened to your voice.
You put down the distractions,
Once and for all.
You stand in your power,
After your fall.
This fall,
Brought you down.
As you grabbed all your tools.
All the tools you would need...
As you grieve,

The life you should have had.
The way it should have been.
You grieve it all...
Every last bit.
You let the tears fall from your eyes,
As you say your goodbyes.
You leave a world behind...
The only world you knew.
This world of self-sacrifice.
This world that you had to become,
Someone else.
Someone you didn't know.
Someone who wasn't you.
You did it for everyone else...
Until your world came crashing down.
Like thunder and a lightning bolt,
That shot you to the ground.
You fell to your knees...
You needed to grieve.
Grieve a life that you built.
A whole world that you knew.
You would grieve this life,
As you set it all down.
As you laid on the ground...
You surrendered yourself.
You gave it all up...
You put it all down.
You have nothing left...
Nothing left to give.
You're letting it all be...
Be what it is.
It is what it is.

You have reached acceptance...
As you leave forgiveness.
You left the insanity...
Walked away from the mess.
The mess that wasn't yours.
It was never even yours.
You just cared too much.
You carried it all...
Until you had to put it down.
Because none of it was yours.
It was never even yours.
You set it all down,
As you fell to the ground.
This ground you are on...
You form new roots.
These roots that ground you.
Ground you to the earth.
You are grounded to your roots.
You made it through your rebirth.
These roots cannot be taken away.
These roots are yours.
You are you...
You with your roots.

# I Will Stay The Black Sheep

This deep sadness that I have.
This pain in my chest.
Grief I will put down,
Once and for all.
Grieving for you.
This grief that I feel.
I feel in my chest.
This sorrow that I carry.
Generationally,
Speaking.
It has been inside all of us...
It has been there all along,
From generation to generation.
Passing it down.
Ending with me.
I will feel all of this.
I am putting this down...
This is not mine to carry.
I will feel all of this.
This ends with me,
This will be my story...
Ending in glory.
Freedom and peace.
Sitting in this.
Feeling all of this.
Ending this denial.
Ending this illusion...
This illusion covered all of this pain...
That no one could face.
No one wanted to see.

See the truth.
They didn't want to look,
At what was behind their masks.
Behind this façade.
This façade they put on.
They didn't want to see...
This is ending with me.
I put an end to all of this.
This generational pain.
This pride and envy,
That this family carries.
I am setting this down.
This low vibrational vibe.
This vibe in our family,
That no one wants to see.
They want to blame me.
I am to blame...
Because I am the black sheep.
The odd one out...
The one who calls everyone out.
The one who speaks the truth,
And destroys their façade.
The one who mirrors back,
Every single flaw.
Every single flaw,
That they don't want to see.
This is why they blame me.
They want to put it all on me.
So they don't have to see,
This family's history.
So they don't have to see,
What is hiding in them.

I reflect back to them...
Everything they don't want to see.
Everything they shove down,
As they pretend they are great.
As they pretend they are perfect,
As they perform for their show.
Selling tickets to all of their friends.
Their friends that believe their truth.
Their friends that follow along...
With whatever they say.
Because it is easiest this way.
Everything stays the same...
As I become their punching bag...
More and more blame,
Being thrown at me.
Thrown in my face.
All of this envy.
This low vibrational feeling,
That they still carry.
As I clear it all away...
As I walked away...
Being okay,
With being called names.
Being belittled.
Being betrayed.
Becoming the villain,
So they can be the victim.
This is the only way...
For me to stay the black sheep.
I am done fighting this...
I am finally owning this name.
Proud of this label.

---

Proud of this title.
The only title I carry,
As I wipe my slate clear.
No more labels.
No more titles.
I will stay the black sheep…
As I become free.

# I Accept Who I Am

This judgement all around.
This judgement, I feel.
They will judge me,
And I really don't care.
I finally get to be me,
After so many years.
I became small,
Trying to fit in.
Trying to be loved.
Trying to be understood.
Please love me,
If I do for you.
Please love me,
If I silence my voice.
Please love me,
If I become who you want me to be.
I was shut down,
So many times.
I was dismissed,
Multiple times.
The ego hates me.
The ego will judge me.
The ego wants to destroy me.
The ego doesn't understand me.
I don't care anymore,
What anyone thinks of me.
I approve of myself.
I accept myself.
I don't need to fit in.
I don't need to be liked.

I don't need to be validated.
I validate myself.
I will leave,
The second I am mistreated.
I will speak up,
To have my own back.
I shoved myself down,
For far too long.
I am who I am,
I accept who I am.
I am done trying to fit in...
This is me.

# Normalcy

How I felt safe,
My whole life.
Hiding in the game,
Participating in it.
Living a lie,
My whole life.
Living in an illusion.
Living in the denial.
The truth covered up…
I couldn't see.
I surrounded myself with normalcy.
What was normal to me,
Was actually abuse.
This abuse was damaging.
Damaging to my soul.
Damaging to my heart.
Damaging to my light.
This normalcy,
Damaged my being.
Suppressing everything,
Even my voice.
Suppressing my feelings,
Because this is what I was taught.
Keep going.
Don't stop.
Keep doing and going.
Make everyone happy.
Become someone else.
Someone they loved.
Someone they approved of.

---

This someone...
Was who I became.
A role I played,
Just to be loved.
It was never who I was.
This identity,
Fit into that normalcy.
This normalcy I have learned,
Was actually abuse.
What I thought was love.
Wasn't actually true.
Breadcrumbs I accepted.
I accepted as love.
Doing it all,
Just to feel approved of.
Being the best,
Just to be seen.
Never stopping to rest,
Because why would I rest?
I must keep going...
Performing.
Acting in this play.
Playing my role, just to be loved.
Until the day,
I set the role down.
I started being me,
Using my voice.
I set it all down.
I stopped becoming small,
Just to fit in.
Just to be loved.
I set it all down.

This time for good...
I finally became me.
My true self was hidden away.
Because every time I showed her,
She was torn down.
Scolded and punished.
Dismissed and demeaned.
Condescending behavior,
Surrounded me.
This was what I knew,
This normalcy.
Being kicked down...
Became my world.
Being knocked down...
Was what I was used to.
My feelings never accepted.
My feelings not heard.
My feelings did not matter...
This became my normal.
Meeting their needs,
So they would feel pleased.
Sacrificing my needs,
So they were filled up.
Always saying yes...
Trying to be the best.
Feeling responsible,
For everyone else.
Their feelings matter,
More than mine.
"Oh No. I upset them..."
"I called them out."
"I Told the truth,

---

Instead of following the script."
Always participating in one-sided friendships.
Making them feel good,
Building them up.
Validating everything,
So they feel filled up.
Using me,
To meet their needs.
I see this now,
As I grieve.
I grieve the girl,
Who kept me safe.
I grieve the girl,
I became.
I became her,
Just to feel loved.
I became her,
For everyone else.
Until the day,
I set it all down.
I found my own love...
It was always here.
Here within me...
It was always here.
Here within me...
It was always here.
Hiding underneath,
Everything I carried.
I carried it for them.
Until I stopped.
I will continue to grieve,
As I let go.

I let go of it all,
Just to be found.
I found myself,
Deep within.
Deep within the layers.
The layers of pain.
The pain I peeled away,
As I grieve.
Allowing this girl,
Who was always supposed to be.
I allow her to be seen,
As I shine her light.
Tears fall from my eyes,
Because...
This is me.
Hiding away,
For so many years.
Waiting to be found.
Waiting to be loved.
Waiting and waiting...
And here I am now.
Here I am,
With tears in my eyes.
I found the safety she always needed.
I did this for her.
I did this for us.
As I allow her light to shine.
It is blinding the others,
That wanted her small.
It is blinding the others,
That squashed her down.
It is blinding the others,

Who relied on her love.
Her love that she was giving,
As she accepted breadcrumbs.
She found her light,
Inside of her shadow.
And now her light is triggering,
Everyone else's shadow.
Her light is shining,
So she must step away.
Step away from those who are blinded.
She must leave them behind.
She must step away,
From those who try to dim her.
She must do this,
As she trusts herself.
She must do this now,
Because she finally feels safe.
She finally feels safe in her heart.
She finally feels safe in her body,
As she holds her worth in her own hands.
She will never give this away...
Not ever again.

## Her Crown Has Come In

She is done shrinking.
Becoming small.
Staying quiet,
To appease them all.
Everyone's pleased,
Except for her.
Everyone leaves filled up,
Except for her.
She is done with the small talk.
With the interactions.
She is completely done,
With becoming a distraction.
A distraction for them.
To fill up space.
This satisfaction,
That they leave with.
Meeting their needs,
While hers go unmet.
She is done with accepting,
Everyone's actions.
What is best for them,
As she goes unconsidered.
They cannot read the room.
They cannot see her.
They cannot read her.
They do not understand her.
She is constantly explaining.
Explaining herself.
She is constantly becoming.
Becoming small.

---

Because once she takes up space,
They cannot handle it.
They do not receive it.
They cannot hold it.
She is done seeing everyone else.
Being there for them.
Lifting them up.
Fitting into their life.
She is done giving herself away...
Over and over...
Giving herself away,
In a world she doesn't belong in.
In a world she will not end up in.
In a world where she is not seen.
Seen for herself,
Because she needs to meet their needs.
Doing for them.
Appeasing them.
Holding space,
While she gets left behind.
They see her for what she can do.
What she can do for them...
They do not see her,
For who she really is.
They see her,
Through their own lens.
Who is she...
For them?
Not who is she...
Who is she really.
Constantly giving.
Giving herself away.

---

Leaving nothing left for her,
Because it is all about them.
What is in it for them?
How can she serve you?
How can she meet you?
How can she please you?
How can she appease you?
Entertain you?
Listen and lift you?
What can she be for you?
What can she get you?
How can she hear you?
How can she better you?
How can you grow from her?
How can you use her,
To meet your needs?
What if she says no?
What if she stops?
What if she stops giving you,
Everything you want?
A temper tantrum comes.
You are angry with her.
You will fight her...
Get defensive...
And belittle her...
What if she speaks up?
Starts speaking the truth.
She says what's really on her mind...
And it doesn't appease you.
What if she calls you out?
What if she gets up,
When you sit down.

---

Sit down to join her,
Without even seeing her.
Seeing her,
For who she really is.
She can feel this.
She knows this.
She will put an end to all of this.
Nothing against you...
But her time is here.
Her crown has come in.
It is time to put this on.
She will speak her mind...
And it will be very clear.
She is not here to entertain,
Or play the game.
She welcomes the smear campaign,
That you start when you can't handle her.
She steps into the villain role,
As she stops people pleasing.
You can't handle the truth.
You can't handle her.
She is done bending.
Bending for you.
She will speak her mind now,
As she becomes the villain.
She bows down to this smear campaign...
As she puts her crown on.
Her crown that has come in.
She puts this crown on,
As she becomes queen.
She becomes the villain for them,
As she becomes the queen for herself.

## The Door

When you take a different route,
Than the rest of the crowd…
When you form a new path,
Instead of staying with them.
When you do it differently.
Differently than the world.
When you take the risk,
That no one understands.
When you start saying no,
Instead of saying yes.
When you stop conforming.
When you stop fitting in.
When you start using your voice,
To tell the truth.
When you start being honest.
Honest with your words.
When you start being vulnerable,
You will meet your people.
When you take the mask off…
And you say "That's it."
When you put your crown on,
And it's the perfect fit.
When you discover who you are…
It is not who you were.
Because who you were,
Was what society says.
Who you were,
Was who fit right in.
Who you were,
Was who everyone knew.

---

Everyone loved...
Because she was so great.
She met their needs.
And gave them what they want.
She was who they loved.
She was soooooo great.
She became small,
So they could feel big.
She became the love...
That they relied on.
She didn't talk back,
Until she did.
Until she spoke the truth...
And they all left.
Until they couldn't handle her.
Until they heard the word no.
Until they didn't like her,
Because she became the rebel.
The rebel.
The villain.
The one they don't like.
The one they roll their eyes at.
The one they gossip about.
"Oh, she's changed.
What happened to her?
Oh, we don't like her...
Not like this.
We like her small,
So we feel big...
We would rather have her be,
Who she used to be.
She used to make sense,

And now she doesn't.
She used to fit in our box.
The box we put her in.
She used to fit in.
She used to conform.
She used to please us,
But not anymore.
She does what she wants.
She goes wherever she goes.
She rests when she needs it.
She loves silence.
She is resilient.
Resilient,
Inside of stillness.
She is anything but oblivious.
She doesn't miss a thing.
Always aware.
Always in tune.
She feels the energy.
She receives the message,
Hidden under the words.
Words never have to be said,
But she feels the energy.
What is underlying,
She feels the message.
She receives it loud and clear.
And decides what to do with it.
This is not hers to carry,
It never was.
Carrying everyone's shit...
She finally put it down.
None of it was hers...

It never was.
Carrying this blame,
Like it was hers to carry.
She set it all down,
As she found her own way.
She created this new path,
Towards the unknown.
With zero support,
From the ones she left.
She loved them so much,
But she needed to leave.
Leave them behind,
And close the door.
She needed to close this door for good.
She set it all down,
At this door.
Gently closed it,
And did not look back.
She knew if she looked back,
She would feel that crack.
The crack in her heart,
That lived in her chest.
The tears streamed…
Down her face.
When she realized it was time,
To close the door.
She realized this,
As she still sent love.
Love from her heart,
Through the door.
She blew them a kiss,
As she formed her new path.

She knew this new girl,
That she had to become.
She knew she wasn't welcome,
In her old world.
She knew this in her heart,
As she let the tears fall.
Fall from her eyes,
As she shut the door.
She knew she couldn't rise,
From that other side.
On the other side of the door,
She knew she had to die.
She had to leave her old self,
Behind with them.
She knew she had to die,
So she could become.
Become the girl,
She always was.
The girl,
Who wasn't approved of or loved.
She shoved her away,
To become someone else.
Someone for society,
That they all loved.
This someone she wasn't,
Just to fit in.
This someone needed to be left...
Left behind.
This was not who she was...
It was who she had to become.
Become who she wasn't...
So society would be happy.

---

She finally realizes this,
As she lets her die.
She lets her die,
As she sets it all down.
As she surrenders,
And let it all drown.
As she learns to slow down,
And learns not to shut down.
Take up space,
Because she matters.
She is rooted in who she is,
As she sets it all down.
She closes the door,
Wearing her crown.
Once and for all,
She knows she is worth it...
She always was.

## Showing Up As You Are

Showing up as you are.
Exactly who you are.
Being visible in the world.
Showing up without a mask.
Taking that risk.
The risk to be judged.
The risk to be rejected.
But what is worse?
Being accepted and loved,
For exactly who you are not?
Being seen,
For someone you are not?
Say what you have to say,
Without hiding a thing.
This is just how it is...
It is what it is.
Nothing to hide.
Nothing to keep.
Just be who you are.
This is how you go deep.
Past the surface.
Past the small talk.
Past the weather.
This is real talk.
When you hid who you were,
Your whole life...
Just to be loved.
Just to be approved of.
When you did not show up.
Show up for who you were.

---

Became who they want.
Became who they expect.
Become who they accept.
Become who they love.
Sacrificed yourself for far too long.
Not speaking the truth.
Bending for them.
Keeping it all in.
Just so they would be pleased.
Becoming small...
So they would feel filled up.
Being controlled,
While losing yourself.
Not knowing why,
As you shove yourself aside.
Your voice not heard.
Your voice is dismissed.
You are not respected,
Because it is all about them.
Only they matter...
Shove yourself away.
The things you say...
Are honestly offensive.
They are all offended...
By what you have to say.
This is not your problem...
You finally understand this.
This is not yours to take on.
If they think it is rude,
That is on them.
If they fall apart,
That is not on you.

If they can't handle...
Handle the truth.
It is them in control.
It is them living in denial.
It is them living the illusion.
This is not your job,
To partake in the delusion.
Walk away quick...
They repel the real you.
They will shove it right away,
Until you have nothing left.
This condescending behavior,
You are done with.
When they can't read the room,
This is not your problem.
When they can't pick up on cues,
That is on them...
Not on you.
They lack the self-awareness,
That you crave.
You need them to have this,
For your deep connections.
Without this self-awareness,
You won't have the connection.
Without this connection,
You are left with small talk.
You cannot take the small talk...
Not anymore.
You need to show up as you,
No matter what.

---

## Send Love Anyway

Embrace being different,
Time is passing.
Embrace it all... stop bypassing.
Bypassing the truth.
Bypassing your emotions.
Bypassing life,
This is your devotion.
Your conditioning is not who you are.
Stand in your power,
As you let go of it all.
Form new beliefs,
As you live your life.
Living freely,
As some won't accept you.
As they judge you...
Gossiping and belittling,
As you keep moving forward.
As you remember who you are,
Shrugging everything away.
It doesn't matter anymore,
What they say about you.
This says more about them,
Than it does you.
The ones who love you,
Will always support you.
Even on different paths,
The right ones just see you.
Understand you.
Allow you to be you.
Without any judgment.

Without the gossip.
Without the belittlement.
Surround yourself with lifters.
The lovers.
The supporters.
Walk away from the weight.
Any weight that holds you back.
The digs.
The daggers.
The stabbers.
Shrug it all away,
As you face your pain.
Shrug it all away,
As you still send love anyway.
Because that is who you are,
The understander.
You understand,
What is underneath.
Underneath this behavior,
You understand they have their own pain.
Send love anyway,
As you walk away.
Protecting your energy.
This is your sanity.
You allow it all to just be...
Exactly how it needs to be.
Letting go of control,
Because you can't control it.
Letting go of force,
Because everything just is.
Everything is...
Just as it is.

---

# I Just Am

Today I just am.
I am who I am.
I am done chasing.
I need to be done working.
I will just attract,
And go with the flow.
I will just go,
Where I feel I should go.
Set everything down.
There is nothing to chase.
There is no expectation.
There is no outcome.
I am dropping the fear.
I am dropping the pain.
Living for now,
Because that is all that we have.
I am done living for everyone else.
I am done pleasing everyone else.
I am done being torn down,
When I do not deserve it.
I am starting to live for me.
Setting it all down.
I am free.
Today I just am.
I am who I am.
I don't need to be more,
Than who I already am.
Everything will come,
When it is supposed to come.
Trust in surrender.

Trust in myself.
Trust in the feeling,
That will lead me forward.
Trust in my feeling.
This feeling I feel.

## life is full of choices.

Life is choosing.
Life is full of choices.
Choosing once again.
Choosing once more.
Life is full of deciding.
Deciding over and over.
Deciding once again.
Choosing your own hard.
One choice is easy.
One choice is familiar.
One choice is unknown.
One choice is uncomfortable.
Each choice is a risk.
A risk once again.
Choose again and decide.
Choose from your heart,
Not your mind.
The heart will lead you right.
Sometimes it will hurt,
But you get up again and decide.
Decide again.
Do not give up.
Fall down,
And rise.
Sometimes you will crash.
Crumble,
Fall apart.
It is all okay...
That is exactly what you need.
Be a mess and cry.

Let it all come.
You cannot be the judge.
All you need is love.
When you are down on your knees,
Fall down and land.
Fall apart and crash.
Always get back up.
Ride the waves.
The waves of grief.
When you live from your heart,
You will fall apart.
When you decide from your heart,
You will feel it all.
The joy.
The light.
The love.
But the darkness will come too.
The fear.
The sorrow.
The anger.
Let it all in.
When you decide from your heart,
You will break open.
It will all be worth it.
Each choice you make.
Each time you decide.
Your heart is in it.
This is life.

# Make Choices From Your Heart

Make choices from your heart.
Make the choice from your body.
The bodily sensation.
The feeling.
The vibration.
This choice will be beautiful.
The most beautiful choice you will make.
This choice from your heart.
This choice from your love.
This choice from your beauty.
This choice from your light.
This choice fills you up.
It fills you up inside.
Fulfills you.
Lifts you.
Your heart is beating.
Beating from your soul.
Beating from your love.
Beating from your goosebumps.
This sensation on your skin.
Radiating from within.
Beautiful choices.
Beautiful decisions.
Decisions from your heart.
Decisions from your love.
Each choice lights you up.
Lights you up from within.
Radiating out.
Your worth is lit up.

Vibrantly shining,
From the inside out.

## Home

Choices of love.
Choices of light.
Choices upon choices.
Make this choice.
This choice from the heart.
This choice fills you up.
This choice from within.
You feel this choice.
You do not make this choice...
This choice from the mind.
You are making this choice,
That is coming from your light.
Your light is your love.
Your love is your worth.
Each choice you make,
Decides your worth.
You are worthy.
You always have been.
Do not ever put that in anyone's hands.
Your worth is your love.
Do not forget.
Your worth is a choice.
A choice you will feel.
You do not make this choice from your mind.
You make this choice from your heart.
It may not make sense...
To the logical mind.
It may not make sense...
To anyone else.
But you make this choice.

This choice from the heart.
You make this choice from the feeling within.
You follow this feeling.
This feeling will guide you.
Guide you to love.
Guide you home.

## lessons.

Do not wait. Do it all now.
Cherish every single second.
You are not your conditioning.
Find your passion.
Create your vision.
Allow for stillness.
Money is not everything.
Cherish your memory,
This is an absolute treasury.
Alzheimer's takes this away,
As you are forced to change.
Be soft. Be strong. It's okay to be wrong.
Leave behind a legacy.
Build a beautiful identity.
Give love,
But do not be taken advantage of.
Stop sweeping it under the rug.
Deal with it as it comes.
Accept their flaws,
No one is perfect.
Everyone carries baggage,
It is learning how to carry it.
Leave the situation that tells you not to be you.
Ask before you assume,
But also know when you know.
Worth is not what you do,
It is who you are.
Who you are,
When you do nothing at all.
It comes from your heart.

Inside of rest.
Inside of stillness.
Being good and achievements.
Making money and succeeding.
Showing off and proving.
Making announcements and doing.
This is not your worth.
Your worth comes from being.
Your worth comes from God.
This light that he gave you.
Who you are inside,
At rest.
.Wholeness.
You matter,
In stillness.
Pray every day.
Send love from a distance.
Do not ever allow belittlement.
Do not ever be silenced.
The right people will change your life.
Our pain is our greatest teacher.
Acknowledge and lean in.
Listen to your trigger.
Do not allow others to feel big,
At your own expense.
When they want you to shrink,
This is when you leave.
Trust your instincts.
When they cannot keep up,
This is not on you.
End the games...
Say what you have to say.

Speak your truth,
This is you.
You are not here to follow a script.
You are not here to be liked,
You are here to be you.
When it becomes a weight,
You must make a choice.
That choice will be you.
Always choose you.
Send love and peace,
As you show your worth.
Love should not dominate.
Let yourself be led and reciprocate.
If your light is dimmed,
Walk away.
Surrender.
Let go once again.
There is no right or wrong way.
Make it your own creative way.
It does not have to make sense.
Most things do not make sense.
Feel your decisions,
As you make them with your intuition.
Transcendence.
Presence.
Your empowerment.
Your choice.
Your heart.
Protect it,
It's yours.
The truth always reveals itself.
Trust the unraveling.

---

You do not have to prove yourself.
Parent yourself.
This is your job now.
As an adult,
You are in charge.
Meet your own needs,
Stop waiting for everyone else.
Feel your grief,
It is waiting to be felt.
Put down the labels,
Everything does not need a name.
Sometimes it just is.
Let it all just be.
Stop looking ahead,
Be in the now.
The future is not guaranteed.
Write the book.
Start the business.
Discipline and motivation.
Love your body,
You will have it forever.
Let your body lead you,
As it becomes a vessel.
A vessel for your feelings.
Breathe in.
Breathe out.
Let your body move.
Let your body rest.
Let your body feel,
As you put away emotional suppression.
Your body knows it all before you do.
Unlock and accept all parts of you.

---

524 shell.chelle

Be centered. Be grounded. Be true. This is you.
Everything is not a fact.
Make an impact.
Watch how they act...
Behind closed doors is who they really are.
That façade that they wear,
Is fake.
That pretty picture they paint,
Is all a delusion.
Remove the illusion.
Honesty does not need all the glamour.
Genuine and real does not need to be painted.
Lose the expectations.
Never enable manipulation.
Life is not a transaction.
Let love be an expansion.
You are not an extension,
Of anyone else.
You are you.
Do not ever question your own reality.
This is your sanity.
Receive, as you shine in your femininity.
Compassion and empathy.
Individuality.
Your very own personality.
Safety.
Neuroplasticity.
Communication & accountability.
Discernment & integrity.
Authenticity & visibility.
Normalcy & vitality.
Your breath is tranquility.

Brilliantly.
Vividly.
Differently.
Oh,
So serene.
Bliss & simplicity.
Simplicity is beautiful.
Let your love be unconditional.
You are not traditional.
You are so special,
As you rise to the next level.
As you rise with your soul,
As you let it all go.
There does not need to be a goal,
As you allow yourself to flow.
Allowing yourself to grow,
As you challenge everything you know.
Let the judgment go.
What is supposed to come,
Will come.
What is supposed to go,
Will go.
Exercise your mind,
As you let your feelings rise.
Rise so they can go.
Only your soul knows,
As you part ways with your ego.
You are connected to your intuition,
As you drop all external validation.
As you send out unconditional love,
Because...

We are all connected.
We are all one.

## Your Dreams Set You Free

Your dreams are not anyone else's.
Your dreams are yours.
Your dreams may be judged.
Your dreams may be put down.
But it doesn't matter...
When they don't understand you.
It doesn't matter...
When they don't even see you.
It doesn't matter...
All that matters is you,
Make your own dreams come true.
All that matters is,
You choose for you.
You do not choose to impress.
You do not choose to be a success.
You do not need to win.
You do not need to be the best.
You do not need to be on top.
You just need to be you.
You are you,
And there is only one you.
You choose your dreams,
Based on what you need in you.
You do not need to be seen.
You do not need to be the queen,
For anyone else...
Except for yourself.
Let them criticize.
Let them put you down.
Your dreams are your dreams...

---

They do not belong to anyone else.
All that matters is that you are choosing for you.
All that matters is that you invest in you.
Meeting your dreams,
Is your own success.
Meeting your dreams,
Is how you invest.
Invest in yourself.
Meeting yourself to create your dreams.
Creating your vision,
Sets you free.

*Thank you.*
*Sending you freedom.*

I dedicate this book to all of my heart driven people.
To anyone who has had to make the hard choices to
put themselves first.
Each choice was made from your heart,
even if it brought pain.
Thank you for living from your heart.
Thank you for choosing yourself...
but also choosing me as a part of your life.